Tiny Book On
Data & Analytics

Practical and Basic Concepts for Everyday Data and Analytics

Tiny Book, Big Knowledge

Daniel O'Connell

ISBN 10: 9798592054945

DEDICATION

I dedicate this book to my family (wife, children, parents, and siblings). Their beliefs bless me, the support and inspiration they have provided over the years have allowed me to accomplish so much, and without their help, this book would not be possible.

CONTENTS

ACKNOWLEDGMENTS

Over the years, I have yielded so much insight and knowledge from those hard-working professionals around me. Those same people I acknowledge and thank for inspiring me and thrusting me into higher performance.

PURPOSE

This book is an initial guide or "The Basics" for those involved in and interested in the practice of data and analytics. This book is providing context and guidance in the areas relevant to data and analytics. Other books in the series will include a more in-depth discussion on the specific subject beyond what this book covers.

This book intends to guide and aid those seeking best practices and approaches to data and analytics.

This book, albeit small, provides years of knowledge. Our tag is "Tiny Book, Big Knowledge!"

1

WHAT IS DATA AND ANALYTICS

Data and Analytics are standard terms and used in everyday conversations. From the time you wake up to the time you go to bed, these terms are always present. So why do these standard terms mean, and how are they used? More importantly, what do they mean to you, and what value to the present?

Let us commence by defining what data is. Data is facts, statistics, and other forms of information collected for referential and or analytical purposes by pure definition.

We can simplify this definition by stating that data is all information you encounter and collect. These can be print, digital, numerical, human, emotional, and other forms.

In today's world, we are overwhelmed by the sheer volume of data. From the moment you wake up, you are bombarded by data to the moment you go to bed. In fact, at times, while sleeping, you may be presented with data via a listening app while you sleep. In other words, our world is data.

Data's intent should not be to confuse, overwhelm, or be or little or no use. On the contrary, data should present insight that you could leverage to be more effective.

Data onto itself can be identified as noise or points that have no intrinsic value. As data practitioners, our job is to provide value out of these data points. Data can present value to reduce cost, identify risk, opportunities, increase revenue, and more. Data is more than just an arbitrary point of "something." Information is used in business, politics, healthcare, retail, finance, utilities, and more. In short, data is always present and provides insights into what has happened and what could happen.

To define and use data correctly, we must analyze such data. Now we must determine what analytics is.

To make sense of all these data points or insights, we must engage in a practice called analytics or analysis. Analytics is typically ill-defined and misused. Most people do simple reporting for analytics, while for others, it is more complicated.

Analytics or analysis is not just a science or art but a combination of both, thus becoming a robust discipline; analytics is defined as a logical analysis method.

A more descriptive definition would be "The discovery, interpretation, and presentation of data to provide meaningful outcomes, insight, patterns, and perceptions through the use of data."

Analytics is heavily reliant on models, simulations, scenarios, data, and systems. Analytics is typically performed with data from many sources and using specialized software applications.

A key to robust and enhanced analytics is that it is a multi-dimensional data-driven practice.

Analytics is more than merely looking at numbers and data. Analytics provides your organization with valuable, timely insight into what would otherwise be undiscernible data and numbers.

Analytics is a critical part of any successful business because it provides a great understanding of its directions, decisions, actions, and outcomes.

Analytics is a broader discipline that includes "reporting" and "business intelligence." These two forms of data reporting is a form of analytics.

Analytics is a common term used in business but is rarely clearly defined. At times, the term analytics is used as a catch-all. In this case, practitioners, users, and others refer to data science, reporting, business analysis, and data management as analytics. Analytics can be better thought of like a crystal ball for your organization.

With organizations consuming data at larger and larger rates and from many different sources, analytics provides a mechanism to consume and understand such data effectively.

Analytics has many uses across the business, public sector, defense, and other organizations. The usefulness of analytics are endless, and new benefits are derived frequently.

Some of the uses of analytics include:

- Provide insights to an organization
- Identify risks
- Comparison
- Measure and track results on a timely basis
- Forecast/predict future occurrences
- Provide an easy-to-understand version of the

data for users
- Find areas of opportunity
- Identify patterns
- Define and report on efficiency and efficacy

Some of the leading corporate uses of analytics reside in crucial business functions. These essential business functions or operational areas leverage analytics in all its forms to strategize, identify risk, identify opportunities, measure performance, measure sales, and more.

As identified in the image above, analytics is used in many areas of an organization and beyond.

Currently, most organizations have a poor understanding and methods of defining the "true" value or "how" to create value from analytics. Analytics can provide many values for an organization. The values provided by analytics are measurable in both quantitative and qualitative forms. Values include but are not limited to:

- Reduced cost
- Increased revenue
- Reduced risk
- Understanding of behaviors and customers

A fundamental misunderstanding or mistake that organizations get wrangled in is that they confuse data collection with data analysis. Albeit data collection is a crucial component of the analysis, it is not the same. In other words, if you collect vast amounts of data, such collection may not render results. Organizations typically only analyze between ½ and 12% of the data they collect. Yes, this means that only 6 ¼ % of the data collected is analyzed, leaving circa 93 ¾ of the data collected unanalyzed.

There are several reasons why organizations collect data, store data, and analyze data, but at times these reasons boil down to just "Because we can, thus we should." Because we can thus we should is a common statement made by information technology groups, compliance groups, legal, and others across many organizations. In doing so, the problem lies in the volume and quality of the data collected. At times, the data is in the Terabytes, if not Petabytes, in storage. In addition to this and to complicate matters, the data is unclean and indiscernible. For these reasons, organizations then opt not to investigate that data. Beyond those factors, the cost of storage and the cost of structuring that data for analysis purposes are too much for most organizations to manage and use such data effectively.

Ahead in this book, we elaborate on making data analysis more effective and less costly. As a result, organizations and people can leverage the data that is needed.

Keep in mind that not all data is needed. The adage of GIGO (Garbage In, Garbage Out) is one commonly encountered in analytics and data practices. The goal here is to present a format to collect and focus on data that provides value and can be effectively analyzed.

Do not get me wrong, having access to data is great, but the key is data. In short, collect the information you need when you need it. Remember, storage is not cheap. Moreover, as your passion, understanding, and needs grow, your data footprint should grow.

2

CATEGORIES OF DATA

Now that we have defined and explained what data and analysis are, we must now define data types. Types of data are an essential component in understanding the case of use for data and analysis. Data is typically composed of various kinds. Each of these types corresponds to a specific information type and subject.

Why is it important to understand the data type and its purpose? In short, understanding each data type and purpose will allow us to design and build analyses that help us tell a story behind those information points more effectively.

Data types can be encountered in all forms of data or information. Among the most common data types or classifications are structured and unstructured data. These two (2) main classifications of data define how the data or information is composed.

- **Structured Data** – Structured data is defined by the structure or composure of how the data is stored. Structured Data typically has metadata and is quantitative. Structured Data has a data model. Structured data generally is about 20% of all the data encountered. Structured Data is typically found in databases, spreadsheets, and other similar models. This data class can be analyzed and queried by standard query languages such as SQL.

- **Unstructured Data** – Unstructured data is defined by the lack of structure or lack of data model. Standard query languages cannot analyze unstructured data, and this data classification typically is composed of qualitative data. Unstructured data is generally stored in non-relational databases such as NoSQL and Big Data (Data Lake) stacks.

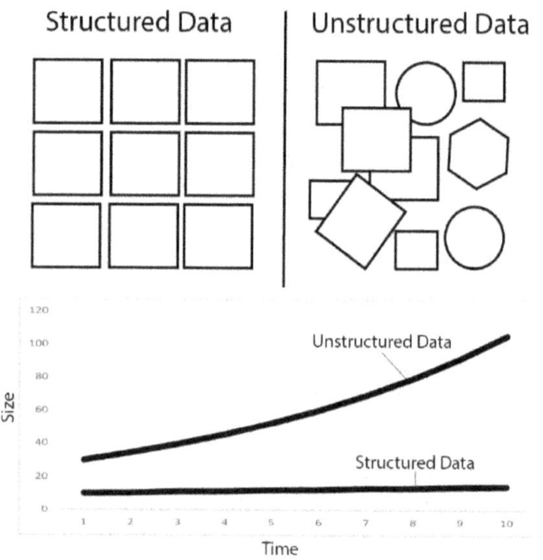

Figure 1

As displayed in figure 1, Structured Data is well organized and in order. Unstructured, on the other hand, does not follow a structure or organization. Furthermore, Structured Data grows over time at a slower rate than Unstructured Data, which grows exponentially over time. Because of the insatiable appetite for data over time, Unstructured data multiplies as consumption increases and new data sources are identified.

Now that we have defined and explained data categories let us now explore data types within those categories. Data categories can be further subdivided into data types that define the data, data use, and value.

The main data types typically utilized by most people and organizations are:

- Quantitative
- Qualitative
- Attribute
- Discrete
- Continuous
- Nominal
- Ordinal
- Interval
- Ratio
- Binary
- Symmetric
- Asymmetric

Each of these data types has a specific definition use case. As a component of these data types, data is collected from a variety of locations and sources. These data types can be, as mentioned before, both structured and unstructured. The value, case of use, validity, security, and accuracy depends on the organization, how the data is collected, and the output.

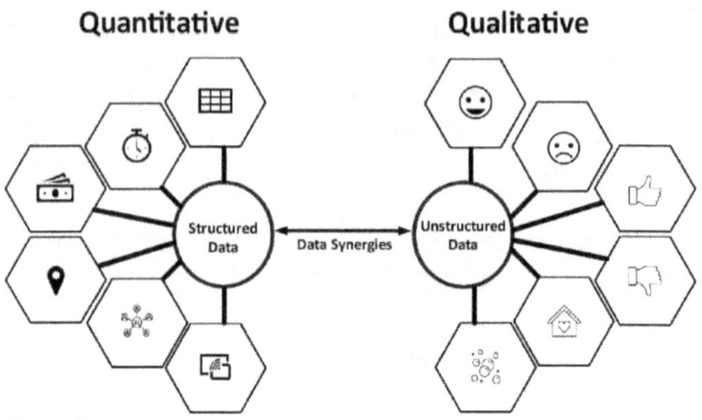

Figure 2

As displayed in figure 2, data is typically composed of the two main types beyond the two principal categories. The two main types are Quantitative and Qualitative. We will now explore in further detail each of these data types and their corresponding subtypes.

Quantitative data refers to data that can be quantified or calculated. Quantitative data is typically structured data that has values. This data contains numbers, facts, descriptive information, etc. Quantitative data is counted, grouped, measured, and displayed using numbers. Quantitative Data is either discrete or continuous and is always numerical.

Qualitative data refers to conceptual data. Qualitative data can be things like sentiments, traits, and other characteristics that are not typically numeric. Qualitative data can be converted to Quantitative by grouping, ranking, and establishing frequency. Qualitative data is generally nominal, ordinal, and binary. Furthermore, binary data can then be symmetric or asymmetric.

Attribute Data refers to data that possesses some form of quality characteristic. For the most part, this data tends to be binary (0,1 or Yes or No) values. Attribute data can also be leveraged as a pass/fail attribute on data. Does item X meet Y criteria? Yes/No or Pass/Fail.

Discrete Data refers to data that can only contain or ingest specific values. There are typically predefined values (e.g., the number of houses on a city block is 2.) In this example, the number is discrete and is limited to a specific value of a whole number as there cannot be fractions of a house in a city block.

Continuous Data refers to data that can contain or ingest any value (e.g., Time to frame a house can be in days, hours, minutes, seconds.) In short, here, the value is not determined and or limited.

Nominal Data refers to data that is used for labeling without a quantitative value. Nominal data is the simplest form of scale in data. Nominal data cannot be ordered nor measured. This data is most typically represented as a classification of something (e.g., gender, race, etc.)

Ordinal Data refers to data that can be ordered and classified. This data can be grouped and measured and expands on nominal data (e.g., what vehicle type you drive: compact, subcompact, midsized, SUV, truck, etc.)

Interval Data refers to data used to represent or display units and the difference between such differences (e.g., What is the temperature outside? -14, -2, 0, 24, 32, 60.) One key to note is that interval data does not have an absolute zero (0.) You can add/subtract interval data, but you cannot multiply or divide it to calculate ratios.

Ratio Data refers to data like interval data. This data can be measured in units or values, but ratio data does have an absolute zero (0.) Furthermore, ratio data is always ordered in units of the same difference (e.g., What is your height in inches? 60, 66, 72, 75, etc.)

Binary Data refers to data where its values can only be in two possible states (e.g., pass or fail / yes or no, etc.) Think of binary data as a series of 0's and 1's where each of those binary values represents a given state or condition.

Symmetric Data refers to data in which values or variables simultaneously occur, and thus the mean, median, and mode occur at the same points. Symmetric data is consistent and predictable.

Asymmetric Data refers to data whose values and distribution occur at different frequencies and with irregularities. As a result, the mean, median, and mode for asymmetric data will occur at various points.

The above data types are essential to understand

and their case of use and definition as they impact how we use them and analyze them. Depending on the data type, we may leverage different analytical and statistical methods to utilize and explore the data.

Not all data is created equal, nor is it used the same way. Each of the data types mentioned here provides unique values and challenges. Individuals and organizations tend to leverage data in a single-threaded method and then encounter the values or output issues. Data, when leveraged and used correctly, can provide great insights. In today's world, with structured but increasing unstructured data is leveraged, it imperative that data and analytical practitioners know the basics of the data types and their purpose of use.

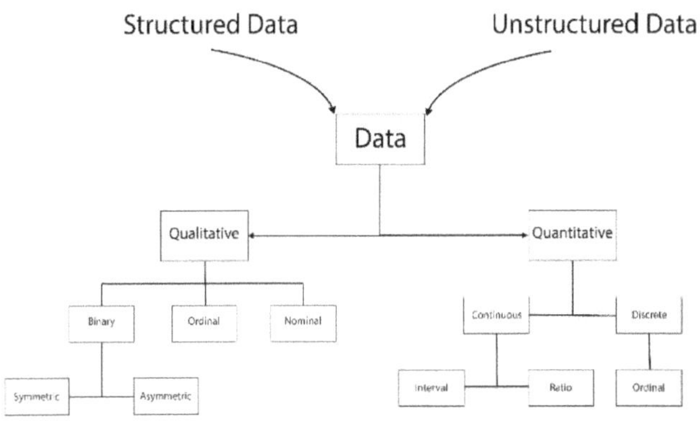

Figure 3

As displayed in figure 3, both structured and unstructured data can conform to the data types discussed in this section. It is imperative to understand these data categories and data types to make effective and efficient use of data going forward.

3

TYPES OF ANALYSES

As is the case with data, analyses do come in a variety of different types. Each type of analysis has a unique case of use and purpose.   The three (3) main types of analyses typically encountered are:

- Descriptive
- Predictive
- Prescriptive

Albeit these analyses are common, they are not the only types we encounter. In addition to the three analysis types, we can also experience the following:

- Diagnostic
- Exploratory
- Casual
- Inferential
- Mechanistic
- Decision Trees

Now that we have named the various types of analyses, let us now describe each.

Descriptive Analysis is the technique by which we analyze or examine what is happening now and what has happened in the past. Descriptive analysis requires the least amount of data and effort to compose an analysis. Descriptive analysis can be in the form of reports, comparative analysis (this vs. that), time series analysis, univariate (based on the single variable), and bivariate or multivariate (based on two or more variables). This form of analysis is leveraged in great frequency by individuals and organizations but provides the least value. With descriptive analysis, you are not performing "What if" or future projects. Descriptive analysis is used when describing customers, analyzing existing sales, census information, school grades, etc.

Predictive Analysis is used to predict a possible outcome. Predictive analysis is based on scenarios and other variables. The predictive analysis leverages descriptive data to expand on such data and analyses. Think of this as a crystal ball for analysis. Albeit predictive analysis is used in "What if," forecasting, and scenario analysis, the outcomes are not guaranteed. The product of such an analysis is further analyzed to assess the efficacy and accuracy of the projections.

This form of analysis does provide greater value in general, over descriptive analysis. Additionally, this type of analysis is more complex to fabricate. Predictive analyses typically are composed of algorithms, workflows, cases, and mathematical expressions to present their output.

As the name suggests, prescriptive analysis is a prescription or recipe of what and how something must happen. These analysis types are very complex and leverage vast volumes of information and complex calculations and workflows to yield their results. Albeit these analyses are rarely used, their impact and value are becoming more and more visible, and their utilization is expanding.

The complexity and level of data used for prescriptive analysis, cost, and time for developing such analysis is always a constraint.

Analysis Value and Complexity

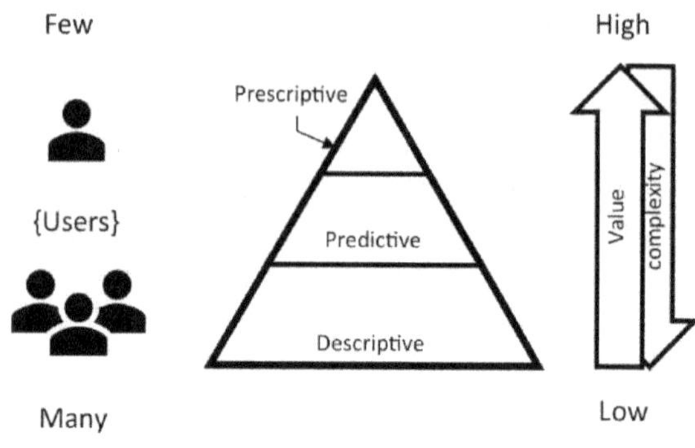

Figure 4

Before moving onto the other types of analyses, it is important to understand value and complexity. Furthermore, it is helpful to understand the distribution of such analysis. In figure 4, you can see the complexity of each type of analysis. You can also see the distribution where descriptive analyses are widely distributed in the same model and have a much lower cost. Prescriptive analyses are by far the most complex out of the bunch and are not as widely distributed. In fact, because of the data presented, the level of complexity, and the value to an organization, prescriptive analyses are typically only provided to C-Suite or executive users and or decision-makers. Prescriptive analyses also require a much more elaborate level of development than predictive and descriptive analyses.

4

REPORTS VS. ANALYSES

The line between reporting and analysis is vague at best. The terms tend to be used interchangeably for users who practice some form of reporting or analytical task. Throughout time, reporting has been synonymous with analysis, but the two are vastly different practices. Yes, reporting and analysis can be used in combination to supplement and or complement each other.

Let us define each to better understand them.

Reports present facts. Data is typically gathered from a well-known and defined data source. Reports provide numbers and facts to what is asked. Reports are generally consistent, repeatable, and highly automated, and inflexible. Reports are typically represented in the form of tabular reports, pixel-perfect reports, dashboards, and the like.

Analyses provide answers to questions. Analyses provide answers as needed when needed. Analyses offer insight not found in reports. Analyses are typically customized. Analyses consider prior occurrences and using scenarios to predict future plausibility. Analyses require human interaction, although new systems are adding levels of automation to this. Lastly, the analyses are incredibly flexible.

Reports and Analyses Comparative Chart

Reports	Analyses
Answers a few questions	Answers many answers
Highly formatted	Provides insight
Highly automated	Highly flexible
Inflexible	Usually requires analysts
Standard Output	Custom

There is an overlap between reports and analyses, as displayed in figure 5. This overlap represents correlated elements where reports merge into analyses and vice versa.

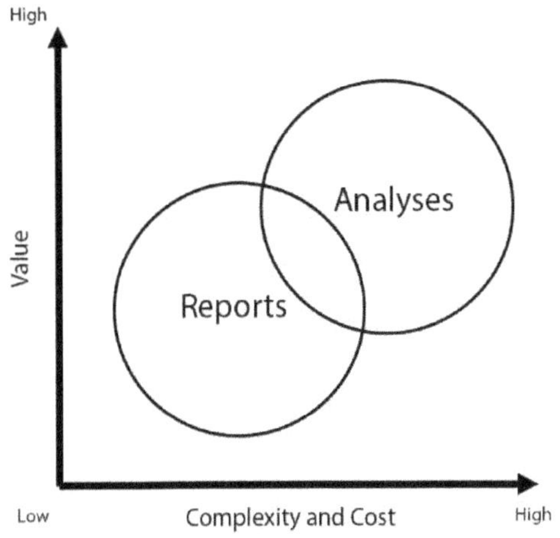

Figure 5

Reports are typically rigid, fixed, and defined where analyses are flexible, answering many questions across many dimensions. Reports generally are highly automated, while analyses usually require an in-depth look at the data. Furthermore, reports tend not to require direct human interaction to interpret the data, while analyses do.

While composing reports, the complexity of fabrication is less intense than that of analyses. Reports tend to be highly programmatic and automated, which can be written by pre-defined queries and scripts. Analysis typically requires more complex development and design and is highly flexible, requiring continuous development and optimization.

Depending on your organization and objective, the decision to use reporting and or analysis will vary.

Here we define some typical cases of use for reports and analyses. You might find that a combination of the two may be necessary to fulfill your objective.

As a rule of thumb, you can define the common cases for reports as follows:

- Repeatable output.
- Many users.
- Highly formatted output.
- Specific outcome or answers.
- Rapid turnaround time.

In contrast, the analyses use and cases tend to be well suited for more complex scenarios. Here are a few of the use cases for analysis:

- Answer complex or many questions.
- Fewer users.
- Dynamic output.
- Complex format.
- More time and budget.

As displayed in the pyramid, reports tend to be more tactical, while analyses are more strategic.

As seen through the pyramid, data maturity and complexity increase with analyses. Analyses provide insight and foresight, while reports typically answer questions for what has already taken place.

There is a natural flow to the reports and analysis process that is evolutionary. This process is typically followed by most organizations when engaging in reporting and analytics initiatives. The process usually commences with standard "canned" reports, which are highly structured and typically answer specific business KPI's (Key Performance Indicators) and then leads into more of a scientific and analytical approach. In the latter, analysts and or data scientists then engage in the pursuit of analyses beyond the reports that provide more significant insights. This evolutionary process is displayed in figure 6.

Report to Analysis Flow

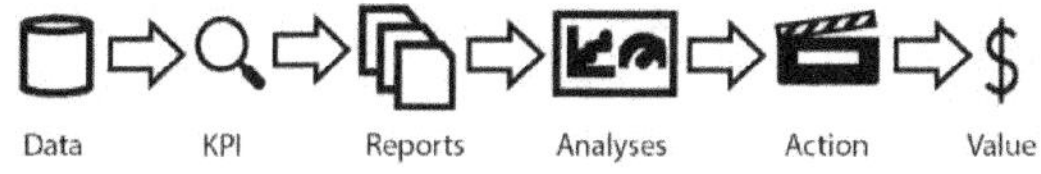

Figure 6

Remember that reports are widely distributed, lower cost, with many users, and many artifacts. Correspondingly, as you get closer to analyses, the complexity and cost increase, but the users diminish. Also, there is no right or wrong answer for which approach or combination of techniques you select. This all depends on your needs, case of use, etc.

5

RELEVANCE OF DATA

Today's businesses generate large volumes of data. Data is generated at a rate never seen before and growing. This mass data includes traditional data from transactional systems and devices, email, open-source, and other forms. Big Data and organizational appetite for data are contributors and challenge businesses who do not know how to consume it.

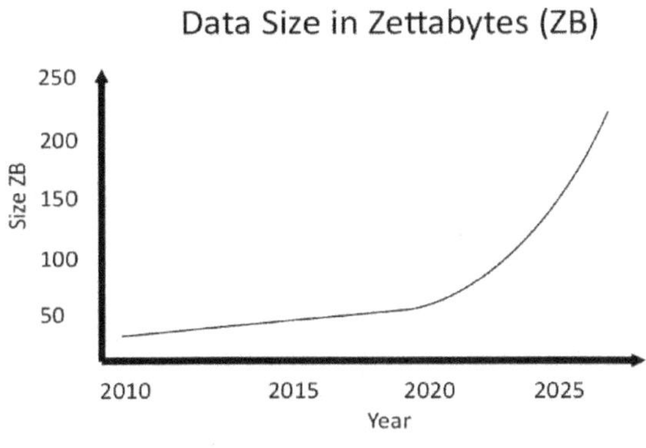

Figure 7

As displayed in figure 7, data consumption has increased exponentially over the last few years, and it is bound to expand more. The data consumption rate now is almost doubling year over year.

Analytics is a consumer of this data in both structured and unstructured forms. When a business does not consume and analyze this data, it presents challenges, missed opportunities, and losses.

Successful organizations understand that to engage in useful data and analytics practices; an organization must take a data-driven approach.

- What Data do I need?
- For what time should the data be?
- Must the data be processed and cleaned?
- Who is going to use the data?
- What frequency should we collect data?
- Should the data be encrypted?
  - At rest
  - In-transit
- How is the data going to be presented?

The above are considerations when collecting data for analysis. Keep in mind that even if the data is for basic reports, reports themselves are descriptive analysis.

Also, individuals and organizations must consider if the data they have had been vetted and adequately defined. This process is part of a data governance approach. (We will discuss data governance later in this book.) The data governance approach will determine the actual relevance of data, the ownership of data, the data quality, the data retention, and the pure definition of data. This definition is typically referred to as "Single Version of the Truth" or SVOT. This concept of "Single Version of the Truth" has been somewhat modified to include multiple accepted definitions for the data. Thus, it can be referred to as "Single Accepted Version of the Truth" or SAVOT.

6

QUALITY OF DATA

Let us begin by defining what data quality is. By pure definition, data quality is the completeness, timeliness, and accuracy of data. A complete description should be as follows: the completeness, timeliness, accuracy, security, and data relevance. In short, if your data is complete and timely, but that data provides no bearing and is not secure, then the data presents little to no quality.

Data quality is more than a technology issue; it includes roles, organizational structures, processing for monitoring, measuring, reporting, remediating, and dissemination.

Data quality onto itself is not a technology only initiative. Data quality is just as much a people and process initiative as it is technology. You and your organization must invest in data quality the same way you invest in product and service quality. This process is very similar to a quality assurance process where you have processes and controls.

Data quality established processes and controls should be tested for effectiveness, efficiency, and completeness. The data quality process should be well documented and defined as well as well communicated.

As part of data quality processes, a few categories should be considered. The types to consider are accuracy, objectivity, authenticity, reputation, relevancy, value, timeliness, completeness, the volume of information, interpretability, ease of understanding, consistent representation, and concise representation, access, and security.

Let us now explore more in detail some of these categories and their impact. The categories we will cover here are:

- Accuracy
- Precision
- Relevancy
- Completeness
- Consistency
- Transparency
- Timeliness

Accuracy is the gap between data and reality. Is there a difference between your number and the actual, true numbers?

Precision is measured as the maximum reciprocal distance between all applicable data interpretations. Think of this as the repeatability given the same conditions. An example of this could be: High is good or low is bad.

Relevance is the closeness between data consumer's needs and data provider output. Data relevance is measured as a percentage of all data required divided by all data provided. In this case, 100% is best. In other words, how applicable and meaningful is the data you are providing to the customer?

Completeness is the extent to which the data consumer's need is met. Data completeness is measured as a percentage of data available divided by the data required. Again 100% is best.

Consistency is the synchronization of data objects across the company. Consistency is measured as the reciprocal ratio of distinct data objects per described object or event. 100% is best. For example, the definition calculates the actual number for an item should be the same across all business lines.

Transparency is the ability to trace back data to its origin and find out its real-world meaning. Completely understanding where the data source is and how calculations or manipulations of data happen is imperative. Documentation of definitions and measures is essential for transparency.

Timeliness is measured as a percentage of processing time attributed to waiting for data. [0% is best] Timeliness is getting data to consumers on time and the timestamps on the business process's data.

What happens when you have poor data quality?

For one, there can be financial impacts such as increased operating costs, decreased revenue, missed opportunities, reductions or delays in cash flow, or increased penalties, fines, or other charges. Additionally, data quality could have a regulatory impact. These can include incorrect reporting to local, state, and federal agencies and industry proctors. In short, data quality can affect the bottom line.

A simple yet effective approach for data quality is performing the 1,10,100-rule pyramid for data quality. The 1, 10, 100-rule, as illustrated in figure 8, shows how $1 spent in prevention will save $10 on correction or $100 on failure costs.

$1, $10, $100 Rule Pyramid

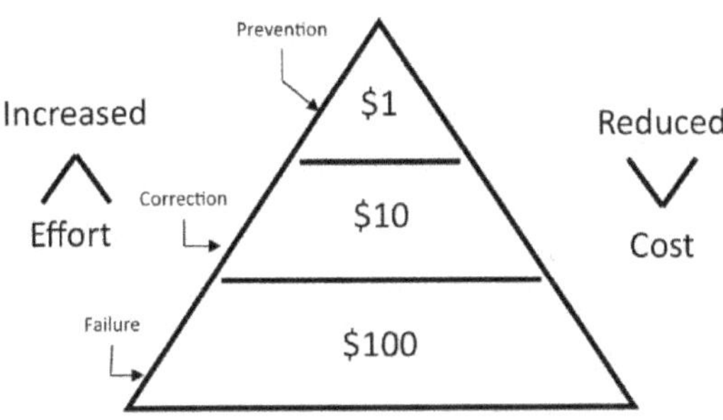

Figure 8

As expressed in figure 8, the cost is increased when attempting to correct data early on. This process has also an increased effort. In other words, when you are proactive in the endeavor of correcting data and ensuring you have good data quality, the cost and effort increases. The goal here is that one ounce of prevention is equivalent to 1 pound of cure.

There are also adverse effects on Confidence and Satisfaction-based impacts, such as customer, employee, or supplier satisfaction and decreased organizational trust. Poor data can also lead to poor decision making.

There can be productivity impacts as bad data can increase the employee workloads, decrease their throughput, and product end quality. Poor data in reports can lead to a waste of time for analysts who need to analyze why they are off and rework the numbers.

There are also Risk and Compliance impacts associated with credit assessment, investment risks, competitive risk, capital investment and or development, fraud and leakage, and compliance with government regulations.

The effects of poor-quality data can then be summarized by:

- Financial Impacts
- Confidence and Satisfaction
- Productivity Impacts
- Risk and Compliance Impacts
- Operational Risks

We have now gone through the definition of data quality and the effects of what poor data quality can do to an organization.

Now let us focus on the possible causes. One key element to note is that data quality is not just making the numbers look good or right. Data quality is an overall symptom of the lack of governance, commitment, and structure in an organization.

Data quality is an information technology issue, but it is an issue of the broader organization. Remember what we said before. Data is one of if not the most valuable assets in an organization. When this principle is not validated, the impact on data quality is immediately visible.

Through the data quality journey, several areas are impacted, but more importantly, some of those areas are also responsible for the data and its quality throughout the entire journey.

A few of the principal areas that are responsible and affected through the data quality journey is but not limited to:

- Technology Architecture
- Data Governance
- Finance
- Human Resources
- Operations
- Marketing
- Sales

Please note that albeit some of the areas affected and responsible are within the technology groups, not all of them are. Each of the areas affected is tasked with defining adequate definitions, cases of use, and data procedures. When data navigates through the data flow journey, ideally, these key affected areas would be active participants (be it directly or indirectly) in assuring that data is of quality through the journey.

One key to note is that having enterprise systems and architecture are not the only proctors in the data quality journey and approach. Technology here should be a facilitator and enabler in the data quality process but not the sole or ultimate arbiter.

As part of the data quality initiatives, data governance should be established. Data governance should also include data stewardship. Data stewardship is nothing more than defining key people or roles who are going to be responsible for defining data, profiling data, and identifying data. Ahead in this book, we discuss data governance further.

One additional component to data quality beyond those discussed already is components that can span layers and assist in tracing monitoring and cleaning issues. These components can also be leveraged as part of a data quality tool kit. Some of the components that can be leveraged here as part of the tools kit are:

- Data profiling and data quality measurement
- Parsing and standardization
- Generalized "cleansing."
- Matching
- Monitoring
- Enrichment

Data profiling and data quality measurement are analyzing data to capture statistics or metadata that provides insight into the quality of data and helps to identify data quality issues.

Data profiling is an essential step in fixing your bad data. First, figure out the extent of what is bad and what is the impact on your organization. Inconsistencies, gaps, and redundancies can all be found using data profiling.

Parsing and standardization is the breakdown of text fields into smaller parts and the formatting of values into constant layouts based on industry and local standards (for example, postal authority standards for address data), user-defined business rules, knowledge bases of values and patterns.

Generalized "cleansing" is the modification of data values to meet domain or other restrictions, integrity constraints, or business rules that define when the quality of data is sufficient for an organization.

Matching is the identification, linking, or merging of related entries within or across sets of data.

Monitoring is the deployment controls to ensure that data conforms to business rules that define data quality for the organization.

Enrichment is enhancing the value of internally held data by joining related attributes from external sources. For example, consumer personal and demographic characteristics and geographic descriptors.

Other abilities factored into the final score are as follows:

Connectivity & adapters are the ability to interact with a range of different data structure types.

Subject-area-specific support is the standardization capabilities for specific data subject areas.

International support can offer relevant data quality operations globally (such as handling data in multiple languages and writing systems).

Metadata management or the ability to capture, reconcile, and interpret metadata related to the data quality process.

Configuration environment is the capability for creating, managing, and deploying data quality rules.

Operations and administration are the facilities for supporting, managing and controlling data quality processes.

Workflow and data quality process support are processes and user interfaces for various data quality roles, such as data stewards.

Service enablement is a service-oriented characteristics and support for service-oriented architecture (SOA) deployments.

As a note, it is worth to mention that we must dispel the common myth of:

"You must have perfect data."

Yes, that concept of "Perfect Data" is a myth. Data is not perfect. It varies and definitions changes based on the case of use and conditions. As a result, the concept of perfect data is a myth, and one that you should not pursue.

A better-suited approach would be to follow the contact of "Good Acceptable Data." With this approach, you seek to use clean, acceptable data based on the condition, case, and situation defined by your organization, regulatory requirements, or other factors.

Although we have discussed the importance of data quality and the effects of poor data quality, getting everything perfect is not always necessary or beneficial. It depends on the data involved – measures surrounding financials and health are probably extremely important. Others depending on the business, may require just directional information. Google Analytics is known for providing only sample data. Also, regarding the cost – if the costs are extraordinary for the last 1% of accuracy, then it would not be worth it. The bottom line work with the business to prioritize data quality initiatives.

7

DATA FORMS AND APPROACHES

Data Analytics comes in many different flavors. This section focuses on the most common forms of data analytics approaches and how data is structured to facilitate data analysis.

Here we discuss some of the common types of data structures used in analytics, OLTP and OLAP, and the subcomponents.

OLTP

OLTP stands for Online Transaction Processing. It is a class of information systems that facilitate and manage transaction processing systems.

Typically, OLTP systems are used for order entry, financial transactions, and retail sales systems. Such systems have many users who conduct short, fast transactions.

OLTP data structures are found in ERP systems, transactional systems such as Order Entry, CRM's (Customer Relationship Management) systems, etc. OLTP is typically a component of ODS or Operational Data Store. ODS is composed of robust systems and databases that capture transactions in real-time and can provide live reports.

In reporting and analytics, OLTP and ODS systems compose the main body of data being reported on. This data is then typically stored in a Database, Data Mart, or Data Warehouse.

Typical OLTP Architecture

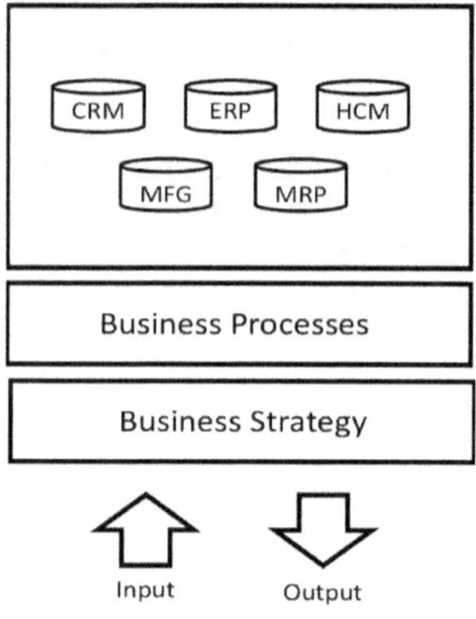

Figure 9

In figure 9, a typical OLTP architecture is displayed. Operation Data Stores (ODS) systems work in an OLTP mechanism for (inputs and outputs).

Before continuing, we should define what a database is. A database is a collection of information stored in a centralized form and container. Types of databases include data warehouses, which typically contain historical data for reporting purposes from one or many ODS systems. A subcomponent of a data warehouse is a data mart. A data mart generally is a small subset of a data warehouse for a smaller subject matter (e.g., HR, Sales, Finance, etc.) and may contain years of data but not typically to the same level of a data warehouse.

In the architecture displayed, ODS systems typically feed a data warehouse via ETL. In turn, the data warehouse then supplies the data marts via ETL as well. For all of these systems, data is typically stored in 1NF (First Normal Form), 2NF (Second Normal Form), or 3NF (Third Normal Form.)

Let us now define 1NF, 2NF, and 3NF.

1NF (First Normal Form)

Data stored in 1NF is typically flattened out. 1NF data means that data reads like a report. Additionally, 1NF data requires that each record be unique (not duplicated.) 1NF data typically has a key defining the record. This key could be a single column or multiple columns. When using multiple columns, that is called a composite key.

Example of 1NF table

Figure 10

As displayed in figure 10, a simple record set exists. To define the unique records, you may need to create a composite key of CUSTOMER, CUSTOMERDATE, and LAST ORDER to correctly identify each unique record.

2NF (Second Normal Form)

Similarly, to 1NF in many ways. 1NF is a requirement for 2NF. 2NF does introduce a new variable that is not present in 1NF. This new variable introduced in 2NF is a unique column identifier, becoming the record's key.

In chapter 10, we will create a table with an ID column and made an identifier and Primary Key. By default, in doing that, we create a 2NF table.

Example of the 2NF table

Figure 11

In figure 11, the new ID column is now the unique identifier and primary key defining the individual row or record. This new identifier can also reference this record in other tables, thus making this a relational table.

3NF (Third Normal Form)

3NF is perhaps the most common data type and structure in use for data warehousing today. 3NF is purely relational, but it is also flattened out. With 3NF, you may add lookup values by using IDs and or other referential elements. Note that this type of data structure is typically lengthy and does consume large storage space.

When most people think of architecting, developing, and using relational data models, the third normal form (3NF) is the one approach that prevails. Albeit this is a relational system, and it is highly usable, this is not the more effective and efficient model for analytical purposes.

Example of the 3NF table

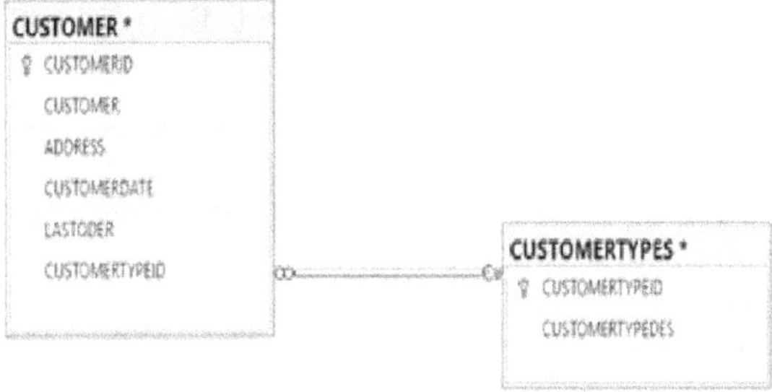

Figure 12

As displayed in figure 12, a relationship is formed between two tables, CUSTOMER and CUSTOMERTYPES. This relationship is between the CUSTOMERTYPEID column on each table.

Albeit effective and easy to maintain, these types of data structures provide little or no value for analytics. These types of structures are well suited for reporting.

Normal Forms of Data and Analytics

The described forms of data, 1NF, 2NF, and 3NF, are widespread. As a result of the commonality, these tend to be the more pervasive forms of data used for analysis. A significant number of data marts, data warehouses, and other forms of analytical data structures (e.g., NoSQL Data, Hive Data Warehouses, etc.) tend to be architected and built using these data forms exclusively.

Ahead, we will explore other forms of data for analytics. These different forms of data are typically best practices for data warehouses and analytical structures.

Before defining these new forms of data, we must first define some commonalities for data architecture and data models. These commonalities of data architecture are incredibly useful for analysis. The most common of these are data warehouses, data marts, and NoSQL databases.

Let us commence by defining what each of these is:

Data marts are data structures or data models that are specific to a subject area of function. Examples of these include Sales data marts, HR data marts, Manufacturing data marts, and others. Typically, Data Marts are a subset or smaller area of a broader data warehouse. Data marts, albeit for the most part a subset of a data warehouse, are not always a component of a data warehouse. Some organizations only have data marts for specific subjects or functions and do not have a broader data warehouse.

Data Warehouses, as the name suggests, is a canonical repository of data for an entire organization. Data warehouses are vast and typically contain thousands of tables, views, and other objects and millions if not billions of records. Depending on your organization, and organizational need, data warehouses can be in perpetuity (meaning that they can contain data for as long as you need it.) In contrast to data marts that typically only have 3 to 5 years of data and are subject centric, data warehouses span decades. They include all the data for all areas of the organization. A common term for data warehouses is EDW or Enterprise Data Warehouse. Here the name enterprise implies every aspect of the organization or enterprise.

NoSQL databases are a form of data store that allows for rapid retrieval of already pre-modeled information. Think of these databases as being in 1NF and with no relationship to other data models. NoSQL databases are used to measure KPI's and answer other critical questions of a business that the data model can be pre-conformed.

The above-noted data models and architectures have existed for quite some time. Data marts and data warehouses work typically in what we call STAR schemas and SNOWFLAKE schemas. These schemas indicate how the data relates to each other.

STAR schema data models consist of one centered table or object (typically a fact) with relating tables or objects (typically dimensions) which link to the fact table.

In a STAR schema, the fact tables typically contain numbers, dates, amounts, and other calculatable data attributes with links to the dimensions via the dimension's primary key, a foreign key in the fact table.

Dimensions are tables that typically describe an object. For example (Accounts, Customers, Products, Facilities, Time, etc.) Here each dimension contains descriptive information about that object. For example, a customer's dimension will have descriptive information about the customer (e.g., Customer Name, Customer Address, Customer Type, etc.)

Fact tables, on the other hand, will only contain metrics and measures. A fact table could be a SalesFact where the fact table contains the product id, customer id, amount of sale, total number of units sold, date of purchase, etc.

These tables work together in a STAR SCHEMA format and are highly effective.

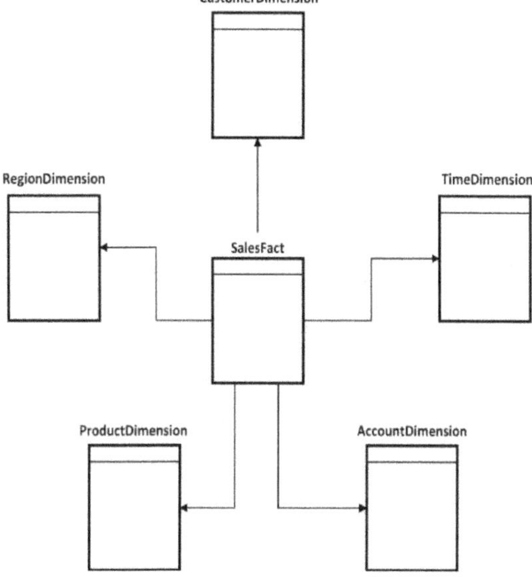

Figure 13

Figure 13 shows the base diagram of a STAR SCHEMA where 5 dimensions connect to one fact table.

Expanding on STAR schemas, another standard model is SNOWFLAKE schemas. SNOWFLAKE, as the name implies, has multiple links, just as a real snowflake would. With SNOWFLAKE schemas, the dimensions are further linked to each other. SNOWFLAKE goes beyond the STAR. Furthermore, SNOWFLAKE can link multiple facts together beyond numerous dimensions together.

SNOWFLAKE schemas are useful at times but tend to be very hard to manage. Additionally, SNOWFLAKE schemas do not lend themselves well for most analytical applications as these applications genuinely thrive in a STAR schema format.

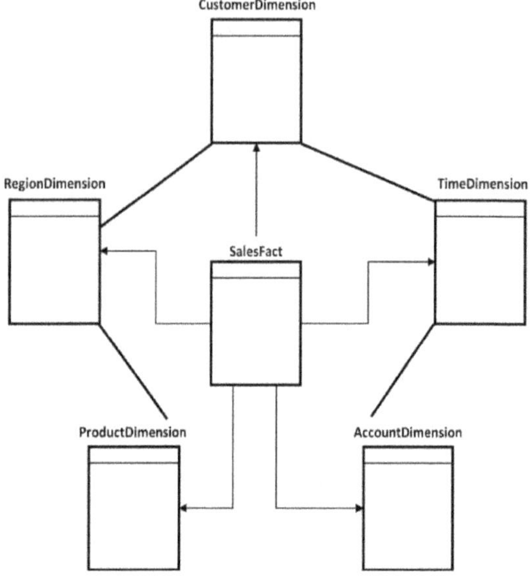

Figure 14

Figure 14 shows a SNOWFLAKE schema. As you can see, the SNOWFLAKE expands on the STAR by linking the dimensions together. This key linkage between tables is a crucial attribute of SNOWFLAKE models.

Now that we have spoken about databases and schema models let us now discuss what is optimal for analysis. As we defined previously, data marts and data warehouses are optimal for analysis. Expanding on that, let us explore the typical architectures for these two (2) data sets. As discussed previously, data marts are typically a level of abstraction beyond the data warehouse. Because of this, the typical architecture for a data warehouse and data marts are complementary. Furthermore, these two (2) data sets tend to leverage the STAR schema approach heavily.

Figure 15 displays a typical data warehouse and data mart architecture with data coming through the data flow from many sources and expending into the data warehouse. As you can see, there is another level beyond the data warehouse that be leveraged.

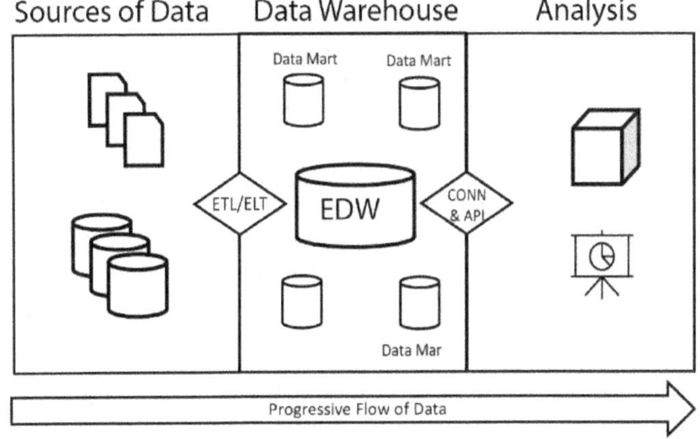

Figure 15

Figure 15 shows the typical progressive flow of data and where the data warehouse and data marts fit. Further, other elements are introduced, such as OLAP cubes and Analytics.

When designing and developing data warehouses and data marts, those responsible must be aware of the process and the schema architecture to leverage. In another book, we will explore further the STAR Schema model and how to develop it further. For this, we will be leveraging a technology called OLAP (Online Analytical

Progressing) in the next chapter. With OLAP, the data model is highly denormalized.

Keep in mind when engaging in data analysis, data-driven practices, and approaches what the key elements to OLTP (ODS) and Data Warehouses are. The chart below will assist in this process.

OLTP (ODS)	Data Warehouse
Operational Data	Data sourced from OLTP/ODS.
Characterized by a large number of transactions (e.g., insert, update, delete)	A relatively low number of transactions characterizes it.
Processing speed is high	Used mostly for reporting (SELECT statements)
Emphasis on speed and processing as well as data integrity.	Processing speed – depends on the query and other factors.
Data is highly normalized.	Data design is highly denormalized and optimized for reporting and analysis.

8

OLAP

Now that we have defined OLTP and data warehouses let us venture into another structure and form for analytics.

This new form is called **OLAP**. Although **OLAP** stands for Online Analytical Processing, it encompasses an analytics and reporting approach characterized by a multi-dimensional data analysis.

OLAP began years ago as a solution to slow reporting against OLTP systems. **OLAP** was done by preprocessing data to provide faster response times. Over the years, **OLAP** has become the fundamental foundation for Business Intelligence Solutions, including Business Performance Management, Planning, Budgeting, Forecasting, Financial Reporting, Analysis, and Simulation Models.

A multi-dimensional analysis of data characterizes **OLAP**.

So, what is multi-dimensional, and what do I do with it. First. Let us define what a dimension is. A dimension is the descriptive attribute of a measure. Examples include Period, Product, Customer, and so forth.

Dimensions can be organized into levels which group members of a dimension based on some level of organization. For example, a time dimension could have levels that roll up from a day to a month to a quarter to a year.

A time dimension, for example, may have

members for each element. These elements could define the levels and cardinality within the dimension, such as year, quarter, month, day or 2020, Q1, January, February, etc., where each month is a cardinal member.

Measures are the data values that are analyzed and can be calculated and summarized. These are usually numeric. Examples of these are the sales amount or count.

In **OLAP,** many dimensions work together to support analysis, thus multi-dimensional. These dimensions work in the form of a cube. The cube is usually derived from a subset of a data warehouse. Unlike relational databases that use two-dimensional data structures (often in columns and rows in a spreadsheet), **OLAP** cubes are logical, multidimensional models with numerous dimensions and data levels. Also, an organization typically has cubes for different types of data. Think of an **OLAP** cube like a spreadsheet pivot with multiple dimensions.

In figure 16, a 3-dimensional cube is displayed. The cube's dimensions are Regions, Products, and Year. The measures are embedded within each section of the cube. In this case, they are the blue areas within the cube. Furthermore, a smaller partitioned cube can be enabled from this primary cube. A partitioned cube is a concept of a smaller subset of the larger cube. Partitioned cubes work much the same way as data marts do with data warehouses.

OLAP Cube

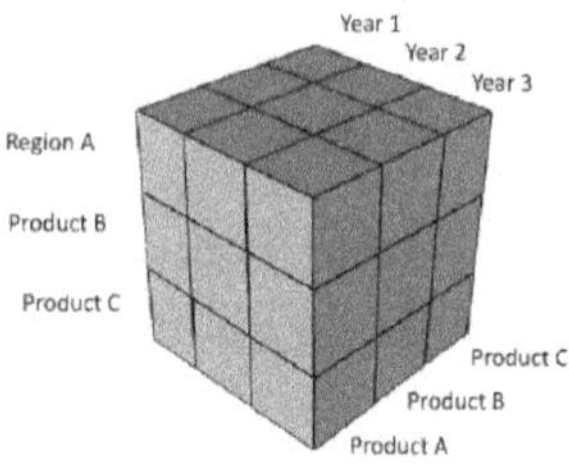

Figure 16

Interacting with cubes can be termed as "slicing and dicing." When you slice, you select a single member of a dimension, thereby filtering on that member – this creates a new cube with smaller dimensions. So, in the example of the previous cube, you can select the year 2014.

When you dice, you are selecting specific values. For example, in the CITY dimension, you are selecting Chicago, Dallas, and Louisville.

Drilling up or down is involved when levels break up a dimension, so for example, if the year dimension had months and days, you could drill down on a particular year, then display all the months, then select a month and drill to a specific day.

OLAP is also grouped into three types or versions of **OLAP. MOLAP**, **ROLAP**, and **HOLAP**.

MOLAP stands for Multi-dimensional **OLAP**.

MOLAP is the most traditional OLAP storage form since its pre-computes many of the aggregates of its data. It also uses a dimensional model.

Some Examples of **MOLAP** engines include Oracle Essbase, SQL Server Analysis Services, and SAS Cubes.

Advantages of MOLAP

- Provide fast query performance due to optimized storage as well as multidimensional indexing and caching.
- Smaller size on physical disk of data compared to data stored in relational databases.
- Automated computation of higher levels of aggregate data.

Disadvantages of MOLAP

- Within some **MOLAP** solutions, preprocessing can be quite long.
- **MOLAP** tools traditionally have difficulty querying models with dimensions with very high cardinality. An example of this is one with millions of members.
- Some **MOLAP** products have difficulty updating and querying models. It requires additional investment in tools and training.

ROLAP stands for Relational **OLAP**. Relational because the underlying data in this model is stored in a relational database. Unlike its sibling **MOLAP**, **ROLAP** does not require the pre-computation and storage of data. Additionally, **ROLAP** can be developed in a traditional database. When building a data warehouse, you can derive many advantages of building your data warehouse in **ROLAP** structures over OLTP 3NF.

Advantages of ROLAP

- More capable of handling large data volumes, especially with dimensions of high cardinality. **ROLAP** makes this option more flexible as more dimensions can be used typically than with **MOLAP**.
- Can leverage all other functionality with relational databases.
- Can join with multiple attribute tables.
- Provides load times are generally faster and more customizable.
- More tools can access it than **MOLAP**.

Disadvantages of ROLAP

- Slower than **MOLAP**.
- Faster performance achieved by aggregation tables, but ETL involved.
- Must involve SQL for all calculations, so it is not suitable for more complex models such as MDX.

Lastly, within the **OLAP** framework, there is **HOLAP**. **HOLAP** stands for Hybrid Online Analytical Processing.

HOLAP is a combination of **MOLAP** and **ROLAP** implementation. **HOLAP** leverages some of the advantages of the other **OLAP** versions. **HOLAP** allows for storing part of the data in **MOLAP** and part of data in **ROLAP**.

Different types of **HOLAP** structures can include:

- Vertical partitioning with aggregations in **MOLAP** and detail in **ROLAP**.
- Horizontal partitioning with some slices across a dimension such as time in **MOLAP** and others in **ROLAP**.

Advantages of HOLAP

- Aggregations queried with little detailed data, **HOLAP** offers fast performance with low storage requirements – just like **ROLAP**.
- The cubes are smaller because detailed data is relational.
- In processing times or pre-calculation are faster than **MOLAP** since only aggregations are stored.

Disadvantages of HOLAP

- As slow as **ROLAP** when accessing detailed data or data not stored in **MOLAP** and processing aggregations when newly inserted records.

So now begs the question, when do you use **OLAP**? Using **MOLAP** or **HOLAP** is dependent on your requirements.

1. Do you need to create multiple slices of multi-dimensional data?
2. Do you need drill-down capability?
3. Do you need fast performance on numbers 1 and 2?

Then taking all the advantages and disadvantages into consideration, the answer should present itself to you.

ROLAP is a bit more flexible in the sense that your underlying structures simply need to be dimensional - having a fact table with dimensions or attributes. However, since generally, the data at the upper-level aggregations are not pre-calculated, drilling and upper-level aggregations can be slow. Some vendor solutions permit the ability to use the aggregate tables to assist in this. Still, generally, you need to know the level at which you want to aggregate before retrieval. If you are reporting on various attributes simultaneously (more than 12 or so), relational reporting may be better suited.

Standard OLTP reporting is generally frowned upon since it might interfere with your production system performance. One solution to this is to mirror the OLTP system using replication mechanisms. This way, real-time operational type reports can be feasible.

Worth mentioning that **OLAP** does have a component of slowly and rapidly changing dimensions. What do we mean by slowly and rapidly?

Slowly Changing Dimensions – Data in a slowly changing dimension is stored in both current and historical form. This data changes over time, but the change is infrequent.
Rapidly Changing Dimensions – Just as with slowly changing dimensions, data is stored for both current and historical. Unlike slowly changing, the

data here changes frequently and rapidly. The speed by which it changes can vary but typically daily, if not more regularly.

Additionally, **OLAP** requires that the data be stored in one or many of the following data types. Type 0, type 1, type 2, type 3, type 4, or type 6.

Type 0 data – This data never changes, and the values persist. Consider this the original data.

Type 1 data - Here, data changes, but the previous record is overwritten when it does.

Type 2 data – Type 2 data retains the original records as captured in type 0 and keeps the new record or difference. Type 2 data is beneficial for comparative analysis (this vs. that or today vs. yesterday.) Type 2 data can grow rapidly, but the benefit typically outweighs the detriment. With type 2 data, a temporal element is generally used to identify the data's effective dates. Additionally, a key or flag can be leveraged to determine the current or most recent records rapidly.

Type 3 data – In this method, the changes are not captured in the same column as type 2 but in a new column or attribute.

Type 4 data – This form of data capture is used in many data warehouses where the historical or previous records are captured in a historical table. Type 4 data typically involves utilizing a temporal table component where a from date and a to date are used to define the data's effective period.

Type 6 data – This typically leverages type 1, type 2, and type 3 together (1 + 2 + 3 = 6.) Albeit rarely used, this can provide some advantages when attempting to capture plausibly unpredictable changes.

Beyond the OLAP types and data types leveraged by OLAP, other OLAP types do exists. These different OLAP types are:

- **WOLAP** or Web-based OLAP
- **DOLAP** or Desktop based OLAP
- **RTOLAP** or Real-Time OLAP
- **GOLAP** or Graph OLAP

These other forms of OLAP, albeit important, are not covered in this book. Lastly, OLAP typically queries or sources by using two keys languages.

These languages are:

- MDX or Multi-dimensional Expressions
- DAX or Data Analysis Expressions

Each of these languages presents a unique method of querying and sourcing data from OLAP cubes and sources and navigating through the complexity of the data's dimensions, hierarchies, and cardinality.

These languages are very similar to SQL (Structured Query Language), used to source data from data warehouses and data marts and ROLAP data models.

9

WHY IS OLAP IMPORTANT

Over the years, the declaration that OLAP is "dead" has been made multiple times. The reality is that OLAP is not "dead." OLAP is alive and well.

OLAP is so visible and alive that Big Data (systems like Hadoop) leverage OLAP via tools such as Kylin. Furthermore, OLAP is used by systems like Power BI, Excel, Microstrategy, Hyperion, Oracle OBIEE, Tableau, Qlik, and many others.

Many systems make OLAP a logical component, not a physical part. Logical meaning that the system builds a non-physical OLAP cube in the application tier, thus providing the full features and benefits of OLAP.

Because of this, understanding OLAP is crucially important. Yes, we know that OLAP, ROLAP, MOLAP, and HOLAP sound funny. Nevertheless, these principles provide an excellent mechanism for analysts and data scientists to consume, parse, and proctor data.

When engaging in the venture of data science, data-driven initiatives, and data warehousing, those involved must rely on OLAP. Ideally, data warehouses should be built in a ROLAP model.

If a data warehouse cannot be built in a pure ROLAP structure, be creative, and attempt some hybrid level. Just keep in mind that because you name something dimensions and other facts, that does not make them dimensions and facts.

Ideally, data warehouses should have many dimensions, many facts, well-defined measures, metrics, and an extensible data flow. These should all be part of an OLAP architecture that could scale.

When building data warehouses and analytics systems, the architecture should be data-driven, not tool-driven. This approach will allow for reporting and analytical tools to leverage OLAP architectures with ease, thus providing you with great flexibility, portability, and endurance.

Keep in mind that when building this OLAP model, a few things should be in place.

1. Dimensions should ideally be built with type 2 data or possible type 4 data. This process will ensure that you have non-repudiable records, and the data is temporal.
2. The data model should ideally be in a STAR schema format.
3. Fact tables should only contain measures, metrics, dates, and numbers.
4. The principle of ACID tables should be in place.
5. Use CDC (Change Data Capture) as much as possible.
6. Generate ERDs (Entity Relationship Diagrams) for each of the subject areas and the broader data warehouse.
7. Use single value Primary Keys as much as possible when possible.
8. Use semantic naming when possible.
9. Identify your facts and dimensions.
10. Establish a data ingestion cadence.

The items listed above are some of the many considerations for an actionable and effective OLAP strategy. In conjunction with data quality, data relevance, and data governance will set you on an excellent path to becoming data-driven.

10

COMMON QUERY METHODS (SQL)

Now that we have defined what data is and what analytics is and introduced some standard terms, it perhaps best to present you (the reader) with the most common and primary method of interacting with data. This method is called SQL, which stands for Structured Query Language. SQL is the standard scripting language used when structuring, composing, extracting, and interrogating data systems. SQL is found in some primary forms such as TSQL (Transact SQL), typically used in the Microsoft SQL Platforms, PL/SQL (Procedural Language SQL) commonly used by Oracle databases, and finally, SQL or SQL 99, which is the ISO standard.

Within SQL, there are four (4) principal sub-languages. These languages have specific purposes and cases of use. We will now define the four (4) sub-languages.

Think of SQL as a catch-all for sub-languages. The four principal sub-languages under SQL are **DDL** (Data Definition Language), **DML** (Data Manipulation Language), **DCL** (Data Control Language), and **TCL** (Transaction Control Language.) These languages do not stand alone or by themselves but are a component of SQL.

Let us now explore each of these sub-languages in more detail.

DDL or Data Definition Language is used to define the data and structure behind the database's data. Standard statements in a DDL structure include the following:

CREATE – Used to create database objects such

as a table, view, and stored procedure, among others.

DROP – Used to drop objects from a database, such as tables and views.

TRUNCATE – This statement or command is used to remove all records from a table in a database.

ALTER – This command is used to change a database object's structure, such as a table or view, but either adding or removing columns, etc.

DML or Data Manipulation Language is used to manipulate the data within a database. DML is perhaps the most common command used in SQL. Common statements in a DDL structure include the following:

SELECT – Used to select or collect specific data from a database.

INSERT - Used to insert specific data into a database.

UPDATE – Used to update records in a database.

DELETE – Used to delete specific records in a database.

UNION – Used to combine queries with a similar number of objects into a single result set.

DCL or Data Control Language is used to grant,

revoke, and identify permissions and privileges within a database. Common statements in a DCL structure include the following:

GRANT – Used to grant users permissions and or privileges in a database and or specific objects.

REVOKE – Contrary to GRANT; REVOKE is used to remove or purge specific user privileges from a database.

TCL or Transaction Control Language is used to control specific activity in a database related to transactions. Common statements in a TCL structure include the following:

COMMIT – Used to commit specific transactions to a database and bind them as canonical records.

ROLLBACK – Used to rollback transactions in the database. Rollback is used when errors have occurred.

Ahead we will explore some standard SQL statements and examples. For the example section, it is best to have a database to test with (e.g., Microsoft SQL Server 2019 Express Edition.)

Sample SQL Statements

This section explores sample SQL statements to familiarize your (the reader) with the SQL language.

DDL Samples

1. *Create a database*

```
CREATE DATABASE MyFirstDatabase;
```

The statement above will create a database called "MyFirstDatabase." This database will be set up with standard options such as full logging and the database's default format, Latin1 General for SQL Server, and the default data folder.

Please note that we are using CamelCase naming here, and at the end of the statement, a commit charge is added. The commit charge is the semicolon ";" at the end of the script.

2. *Use Database*

```
USE MyFirstDatabase;
```

In SQL Server and other databases, the USE statement is an explicit statement to change between databases. In this case, we are explicitly indicating we want to use the newly created database "MyFirstDatabase."

3. *Create Table*

```
CREATE TABLE MyTable (
ID INT IDENTITY (1,1) PRIMARY KEY    NOT
NULL,
CustomerName NVARCHAR(100)
    );
```

The statement above creates a table called "MyTable" with two columns. The first column is an id column with a data type of integer (INT), and it is autoincremented in numbers. The numbers are seeded 1 by 1. This column cannot be null, and it is also the PRIMARY KEY for the table. The second column is a column for customer name, and the column is defined as a national variable character (NVARCHAR) to 100-character spaces.

4. *Alter table*

```
ALTER TABLE MyTable ADD CustomerNumber
NVARCHAR(10);
```

The statement above alters the newly created table "MyTable" and adds a new column called "CustomerNumber," defined as national variable character to 10-character spaces.

The above are examples of DDL (Data Definition Language) scripts within a SQL compliant database that first create a database, second select the database, third create a table, and last, add a new column to an existing table.

DML Samples

1. *Insert into table*

a. *First Option (Single Value)*

```
INSERT INTO MyTable (
        CustomerName,
        CustomerNumber
               )
VALUES ('John',
       '5555555555');
```

First, insert into an example, we table a single value insert. A VALUE statement always accompanies this single value following the insert statement. Note that we must first define which columns to insert into in the INSERT portion, and then within the VALUES portion, we hard code the values to be inserted.

b. Second Option (Select from a table)

```
INSERT INTO MyTable (
                    CustomerName,
                    CustomerNumber
                    )
  SELECT CustomerName,
         CustomerPhoneNumber
  FROM Customers;
```

Our second option to insert values into an existing table is by performing a select statement after the insert statement. In this select statement, you are inserting values from another table into the destination table.

c. Third Option (Value array)

```
INSERT INTO MyTable (
                    CustomerName,
                    CustomerNumber
                    )
  VALUES ('John','5555555555'),
         ('Mary','5545555555'),
         ('Peter','5535555555');
```

With the third option, we can insert multiple values similar to the first option, but now we use an array to separate each induvial value inserted. This separation takes place after the initial value set invoked by a comma.

2. *Select from a table*

a. *Select all values*

```
SELECT * FROM MyTable;
```

With the default SELECT statement, you are selecting all values in a specified table. Selecting all values is done by adding an asterisk (*) after the select statement and before the FROM <tablename>.

b. *Select specific columns*

```
SELECT CustomerName,
       CustomerNumber
FROM MyTable;
```

Selecting specific columns is like select all, but in place of using an asterisk (*), you now define which specific columns you are seeking to view.

c. *Select with conditions*

```
SELECT CustomerName,
       CustomerNumber
FROM MyTable
WHERE CustomerName = 'John'
AND CustomerNumber LIKE '555%';
```

Select conditions are useful when you want to filter a data set. Selecting with conditions is done with WHERE and AND clauses where you specify specific requirements to filter.

d. *Select distinct*

```
SELECT DISTINCT CustomerName
FROM MyTable;
```

Select distinct removes any possible duplicative values that meet the selection criteria.

3. *Update statement*

```
UPDATE MyTable
SET CustomerName = 'Michael'
WHERE CustomerName = 'John'
```

Update statements are used to override or update a current value on a column of a table. When using Update statements, you must first define what table to update. Then you set the column you want to update and the new value. You can specify conditions by which you wish to update the given record. When determining the circumstance, you must explicitly use a WHERE statement.

4. *Delete statement*

```
DELETE FROM MyTable
WHERE ID = '3';
```

The delete statement deletes a specific record based on a condition. In the example here, we will remove the record from the MyTable where the column ID has a value of 3.

DCL Samples

1. Grant privileges

```
GRANT SELECT, INSERT, UPDATE
on MyTable TO johana;
```

The above statement grants Johana privileges to select from, insert into, and update the MyTable table.

2. Revoke privileges

```
REVOKE SELECT, INSERT, UPDATE
on MyTable TO johana;
```

In contrast to the grant, the revoke statement removes any privileges defined for the table or tables. In the example above, the select, insert, and update rights granted to Johana are now revoked.

TCL Samples

1. Commit or rollback

```
DECLARE @today AS Date
SET @today = '2020-11-30'

IF @today = CAST(sysdatetime() as DATE)
    COMMIT TRANSACTION
ELSE
ROLLBACK TRANSACTION.
```

A variable for today's date is created with the actual date value. If the date defined matches the exact system date, then commit the record or transition else rollback such record or transaction.

By no means are the examples here the overall preponderance of SQL statements. The provided scripts are only meant to give insight and samples. Many other statements exist, including REPLACE, CASE, IF ELSE, CAST, CONVERT, and many others.

In a future book, we will explore all SQL language options and how they differ between different SQL engines (e.g., SQL Server, Postgre, DB2, Oracle, etc.)

Again, the examples provided here are simple and do not correspond to the SQL language's full complement or extensibility. The examples provided are to serve as a guide and building block.

11

DATA METHODS & PROCESSES

Now that we have covered many core data and analytics core principles, we should now venture onto some more advanced topics. These more advanced topics play a part in a robust data architecture used for reporting and analytics.

Let us commence by introducing a few key concepts in the preparation and continuous use of data warehouses. The key concepts include:

- Data Ingestion (ETL/ELT)
- Data Streaming
- Temporal Tables
- ACID Tables
- CDC (Change Data Capture)

So, what is Data Ingestion? Data ingestion and transfer is always a critical question that the answer seems to be very broad. In traditional sense-data ingestion is the process by which data is "ingested" or consumed into a data warehouse or data mart. This process could have many different components and mechanisms.

Depending on your environment, data architecture, and other factors, the process could be from something as simple as a pure ETL "Export Transform and Load" process or something more complicated where you leverage APIs, streaming, and processing data, etc.

Let us now define what ETL is. ETL or Export, Transform, and Load is how data is collected and sent to a staging database or server. After this, data is transformed and loaded to the destination or target data warehouse. The ETL process is perhaps the most common data ingestion process, and it is probably also the oldest one.

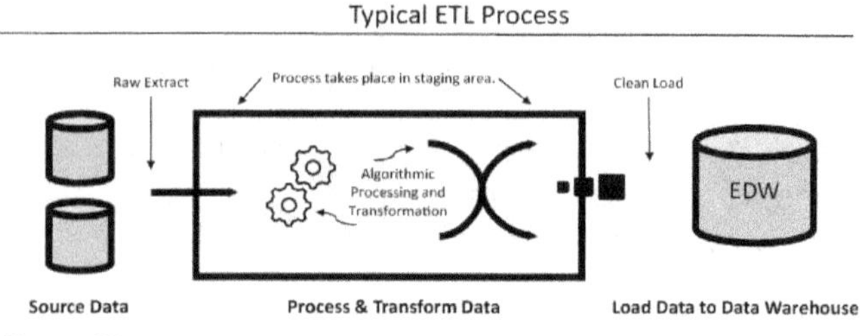

Figure 17

Figure 17 shows the typical ETL. Data is loaded to a staging area (usually a different server or machine) where the data and transformation process occurs. Lastly, the data is loaded in clean, authoritative format onto the destination or target data warehouse.

The ETL process is highly manageable and effective but not typically the fastest. Additionally, there are a lot of moving pieces. By moving pieces, we mean that there are many servers, artifacts, connections, etc., and each of these must be maintained.

A newer method of loading data from source-target has evolved from ETL. This new process is called ELT or Export Load and Transform. Unlike ETL, where the data first extracted, then transformed, and finally loaded into the target system. ELT removes the staging area and performs the transform and processing directly on the target system.

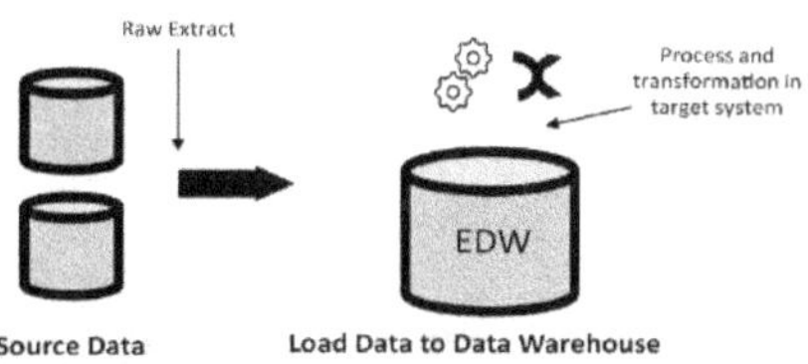

Figure 18

Figure 18 displays the typical architecture for ELT. As you can see, the process is far more simplified than that of the ETL process. Albeit the methods are similar, ELT tends to be more practical and efficient than ETL.

Now that we have discussed ETL and ELT let us now discuss another method of data ingestion. This method of data ingestion is called Streaming. Streaming works like ETL and ELT by taking data from a source and inserting it into the target. A few critical caveats of this are the streaming works in real-time or near real-time. Real-time meaning that data is transferred in smaller batches with far greater frequency (typically within seconds or minutes.) ETL and ETL tend to work on pre-determined scheduled that typically run nightly.

Data streaming is used to collect data from sensors, devices, logs, mobile apps, etc. Data streaming is used regularly in Big Data environments, but it is not exclusive to this.

An earlier version of data streaming was called Pub/Sub or published and subscribe when a source system had a data message. A target system would subscribe to that message at specific frequencies or targeted events.

Typical Data Streaming Architecture

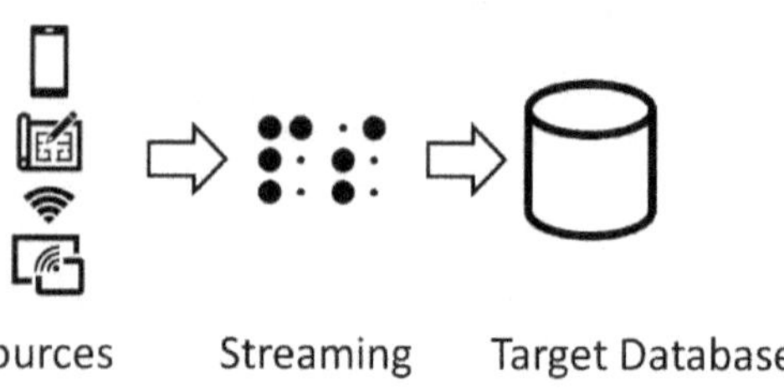

Figure 19

Figure 19 shows a typical data streaming architecture where data is sourced from many systems, devices, etc., and then streamed to a target data system.

Another critical element or method when building a scalable data system, specifically one to be used by analysts and data scientists, is the concept of temporal tables.

So, what are temporal tables? Temporal tables are a user type table that is specifically structured to keep the historical track of data. This process is typically done by add two (2) specific columns to the given table. The two (2) columns added are date_from and date_to or some other modality of the like. These two (2) columns allow for the record to be time stamped. When time stamping the data, you ensure that you define an effective timeframe the data is valid or effective.

Other temporal table options include adding a current_record or current_version flag, which defines which is the most recent record or current record.

Temporal tables are beneficial for various reasons. The principal reason for temporal tables is to keep historical track of data. Historical data is useful if the records, coding system, and other modalities on the data have changed over time. When using a temporal table, another critical attribute or benefit is the ability to do a comparative analysis of the same record over time.

One key element to be aware of with temporal tables is that records grow and impact size on a database. Because you are keeping many versions of the record over time, the data volume does increase. Yes, that is a concern, but we must weigh the benefit vs. cost.

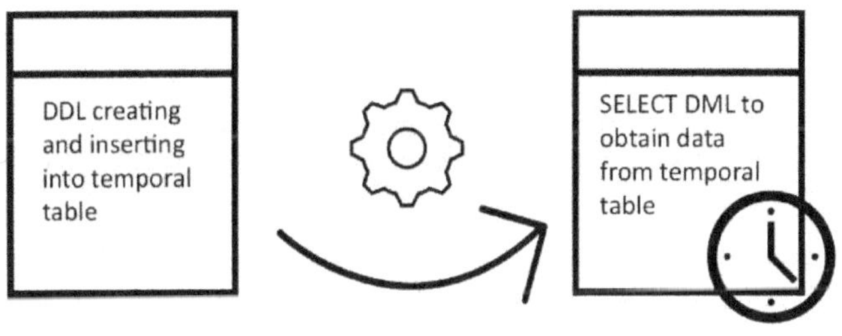

Figure 20

Figure 20 displays the typical process by which data is first inserted, updated, etc., into a temporal-defined table with date fields. Following the insertion of records into a temporal table, a DML script (typically a select statement) pulls data from that temporal table based on dates or current records.

Now that we have covered ETL/ELT and temporal tables, another critical aspect to account for is the concept of ACID tables. No, the ACID, in this case, does not mean the tables are toxic or will destroy other tables, but in turn, ACID refers to Atomicity, Consistency, Isolation, and Durability. In ACID tables, the key characteristics are that the tables are guaranteed data validity. ACID is done by effectuating the processes mentioned above.

Atomicity refers to the integrity of the data itself. Integrity refers not only to transactions all aspects of a table and record.

Consistency refers to the overall reliability of every transaction inserted into the database table. In this case, the data written is consistent and meets the criteria that define such consistency.

Isolation refers to each transaction leaves the data in the same state or condition it was and ensuring the transaction is completed successfully.

Lastly, durability is there to guarantee that the data has been appropriately committed and persist.

If there is a failure in any ACID transaction spot, the transaction is not completed; thus, the record is then not inserted and guarantees overall cohesion to durability, quality, and completeness.

Just as crucial for a scalable enterprise data system supporting analytics and reporting is CDC's concept (Change Data Capture.) Change Data

Capture is nothing new. In short, what this process does is ensure that only changes have from the previous record load are loaded. CDC is typically done via several mechanisms, including complex SQL statements as well as via tools.

CDC works in conjunction with ACID processes as well as temporal methods. CDC is typically part of the ETL/ELT data ingestion mechanism.

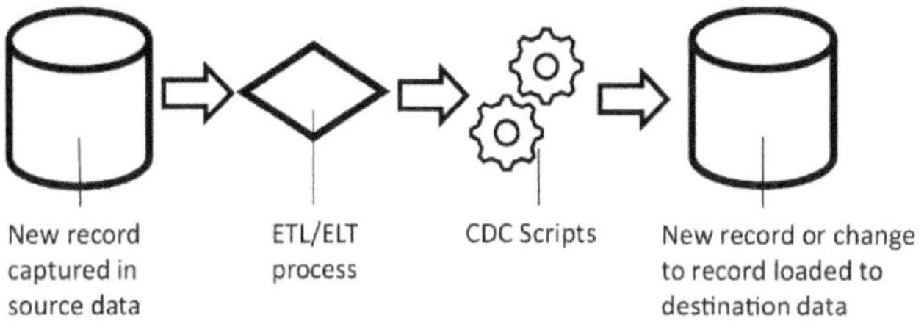

Figure 21

Figure 21 displays the typical CDC process effectuated. This process commences with data at the source. CDC begins as part of the ETL/ELT process with some conditions and or scripts to effectuate the CDC itself and then load the changes or new record to the target database.

The above areas could leverage additional data and analytics concepts that provide great value and assist in mature analytics and data practice development and growth.

12

DATA SECURITY

Data security seems to be a complex and daunting topic. The reality is that, albeit complex, security need not be daunting. Data security should always be a critical aspect of a data project and the data conversation. This book will cover some of the critical elements of data security and why they are essential.

So, where to start with data security? That always seems to be the question at hand. Depending on who you talk to or leading a data project, this topic can take different directions.

At the core of data security, the questions should always be first and foremost as follows:

1. What data do we need?
2. Is the data company confidential?
3. Who will be the intended users?
4. What is the frequency and mechanism of distribution and consumption?
5. Is the data affected by governmental rules (federal, state, local)?
6. Should the data be encrypted?
7. How do we identify potential risks and breaches?
8. How do we recover from a breach?

The above questions are not all the questions to ask or all areas of consideration, but these serve as a starting point for data security conversations.

The first order in the process should always be what data we need to whatever the requirement is. Here, the first is to assess what data is truly needed. Keep in mind that not all data is first required and second necessary. Once you have asserted what data you need, then you proceed with a few other considerations such as:

1. Do we already have this data?
2. Are there rules or regulations that pertain to or affect this data?
3. Where is the data stored if we already have it?

Following the data need question, you should proceed to evaluate then if this data is confidential. Now, let us expand on if the data is confidential or not. In some organizations, not all have data security classifications that govern how the data is stored, distributed, and consumed. Depending on your organization, this may already exist, or it may not. For some organizations, data is typically categorized into three (3) main categories depending on the data type. The three (3) main data types based on security classifications are typical:

1. Public
2. Private
3. Confidential

Public data refers to data commonly available in the public domain and does not risk the organization.

Private data refers to data that, albeit not governed or proctored by statutory requirements, such data may present a risk for the organization. Data of this type may be salaries, expenditures, some types of metadata, etc.

Confidential data refers to data that will have a

significant risk and impact on the organization. This type's data is of strict confidence, and it could be controlled by NDA's (Non-Disclosure Agreements) and other stipulations. This data is typically governed also by governmental and or industry regulations.

If your organization does not follow a process like the one above to define data, your data and analytics project may be a great way to initiate the conversation and implement such an initiative.

Now that you have assessed which data is needed and is the data confidential, the other important consideration is to define who are the intended users.

When defining who are the intended users, ensure that you indicate who they are, why they need the data, and the frequency by which they will consume the data. As part of this initiative, you should keep a running list of those who will use the data. One key element to remember is that most people will always want access to data, but they will not articulate why they needed.

It is imperative that as you define who will use the data, you also specify the case of use or why they needed the data. Specific definitions will give validity and justification for such use.

Once you have defined who will use the data, the other critical component for data security is the data frequency. By frequency, we mean when users will use the data and when they are collected and processed. Frequency is critical as untimely data can present a challenge and, at times, present erroneous results or outputs.

Expanding on this, you should also explore how the data will be consumed, such as the data presented via a report, dashboard, email, API, etc. As part of that, then the consideration should be if there should be additional checks and balances. For example, suppose the data is to be rendered via a dashboard. In that case, typically, you can track usage of the dashboard and present the users with authentication and authorization challenges that ensure that the specified user is the correct one.

Systems such as reporting and analytics systems typically have logs that track the who, what, when, where, and how. Logs present a great way to non-reputable track usage and assess if miss use of unintended use has taken place.

Other mechanisms could include MFA (Multi-factor Authentication), token usage, and others to present challenges and only allow specific users to access the data.

Further considerations for data security include assessing the impact of data to an organization, the value of data, the criticality of data, etc.

Following well-established frameworks, a mature data practice should also include concepts of data privacy and governance. Examples of this include identifying internal and external requirements, impact assessments and analyses, segregation of duties and responsibilities, reporting on current and plausible future statuses, and more.

Other areas to consider for data security include the architecture and privacy and the lifecycle of the data.

13

DATA GOVERNANCE

Data governance always appears to be big and untenable when it comes to data and analytics projects. The reality is that data governance should be a crucial and integral part of a data and analytics practice.

The concept of governance should be fluid and well established. Organizations should define a process for their data governance.

First, we must define the purpose of data governance. Data Governance intends to steer and align data use strategies, data quality, data stewardship, and data use across the organization. Data Governance is a facilitator for becoming a data-driven organization.

Data is an asset. Use it and place value on it adequately.

To proceed with this, you must do the following:

- **Establish stakeholders** – These are the people who are responsible for the data. They are the data owners. In short, these are the ones who are accountable for the data.

- **Establish policy and definitions** – This is the method by which to process, consume and proctor data. Policies should be well documented and repeatable.

- **Establish stewardship and** stewards – This is the process and methods and the people's actions on data. They report to and are accountable to the stakeholders.

- **Define risks and mitigation** – This is the process that assesses any plausible risk and the mitigation or counter actions in the event of risk or failure.

- **Leverage technology** – Use all available technology and systems to accomplish proper data governance.

- **Establish timelines** – This is the time it will take to take any action or do something. In a proper data governance process, there is always a timeframe. Timelines are crucial as data is fluid and never stale. Furthermore, definitions, actions, and effects are still time-based and variable.

The principal goal of data governance is to ensure that data is consistent and trusted. Additionally, data governance helps use data to make effective and efficient decisions on a timely basis, thus increasing profits and reducing costs.

So, where does data governance fit? Data governance plugs into a broader data systems framework, as displayed in figure 22.

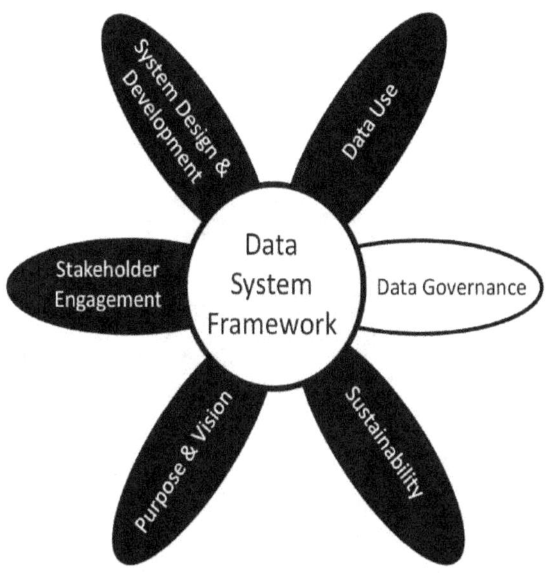

Figure 22

Furthermore, the data governance process should include data for all critical aspects of the organization. This process should be inclusive and not exclusive. In image 23, an example of data governance areas of including is displayed.

Figure 23

Data governance intends to enable organizations to be agile, precise, effective, and, most importantly, data-driven. As part of this endeavor, organizations must engage in continuous improvement processes to continuously evolve and optimize.

The process of becoming data-driven as part of a data governance initiative will allow such organizations to:

- Provide trusted data
- Provide a 360° view of the organization
- Tell a story being the data
- Be visual and compelling
- Provide accurate historical data
- Provide easy to understand insights

Of course, there are always some challenges for engaging in data governance. Perhaps the most challenging aspect of data governance is adhesion and cultural change. Once a change or process is established, there will always be some level of challenge or apprehension. Be mindful of this. In figure 24, a diagram shows some of the most likely elements of the challenge. These elements are around people. Recognize those and work around them.

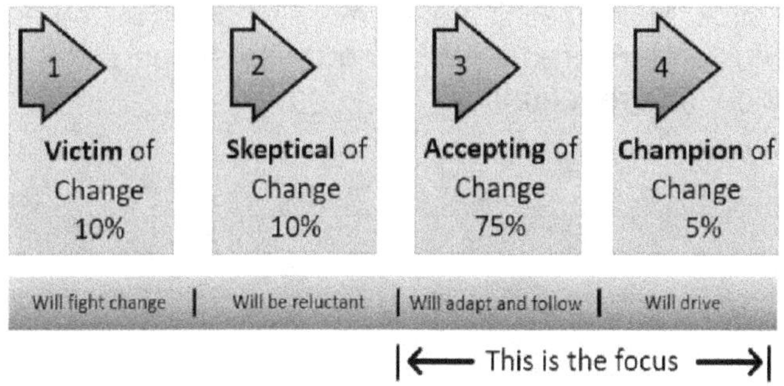

Figure 24

To effectively implement data governance, focus on the champions and those accepting change. Do not focus on the victims of change or the skeptical of change. When focusing on the latter two (2), the odds will always be against you. This focus will harm data governance efforts.

Now that you understand the purpose and who to engage for a genuinely successful data governance initiative, the next step is to define the steps on how to get there. The steps are seven simple steps that are self-explanatory.

1. Create Urgency
2. Find Allies
3. Provide a Clear Vision of the Future
4. Make it Known
5. Empower
6. Have Quick Wins
7. Build on It

Figure 25 shows the seven steps, which presents them in a linear approach. Also, remember to make it stick. Make it stick means merely having an impact and remembered. Following these seven steps, it should be repeatable.

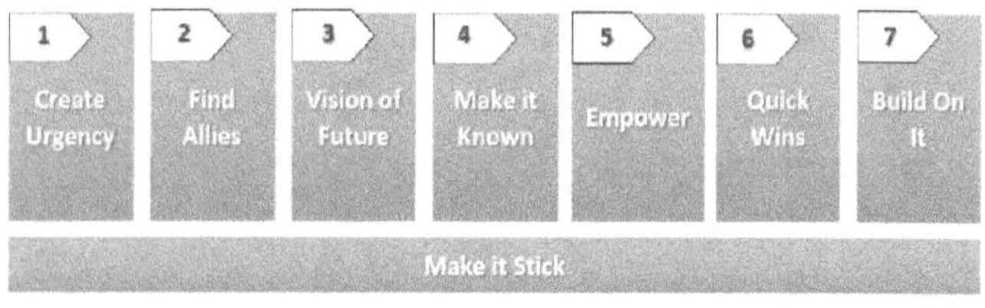

Figure 25

Lastly, for data governance, be aware of possible barriers such as technology barriers (e.g., software, systems, etc.) and non-technology barriers (e.g., silos, gatekeepers, false-promises, etc.) Be aware there is no such thing as a "Golder Ticket" and no perfect "Promise Land."

If you recognize these and follow the steps described here, you should be in a good position for a successful data governance engagement.

14

BIG DATA

Big data is a subject that you cannot move away from these days. We have discussed data and processes for data, but how do these apply to big data? First, we must define big data and its relevance to the overall world of data and analysis.

Big data seems like a magical thing at the time. It may seem that, as the name indicates, it is so big that it is unmanageable. Big data is not as complicated as the name suggests.

Let us commence by defining big data and how it is a part of analytics and the overall data ecosystem. Big data is so large in volume that it cannot be processed or structured with traditional data systems. So, what does the term "so large" mean? So large means that the data comes in large volumes. Typically, in gigabytes, terabytes, and petabytes. Additionally, the data tends to be unstructured, as discussed in a previous chapter unstructured, meaning without the traditional metadata that defines columns, rows, and other attributes.

Big data is typically stored in non-relational systems such as Hadoop, Azure Big Data, Amazon Big Data, Google Big Query, etc. These systems tend to store the data in similar ways on cloud-based systems across multiple compute nodes (servers.)

Albeit big data is typically cloud-based, the cloud could be a hybrid cloud of a public cloud (e.g., in a public system such as Azure, AWS, Google, etc.) or on your cloud or private cloud in your data center.

Big data is stored in what is typically referred to

as a data lake. A data lake is nothing more than a reservoir or collection of massive amounts of data ready for discovery. Data lakes can be in many flavors and sizes. At times poorly managed data lakes become data swamps.

Yes, big data is loaded with unclean, unmanaged data ingested directly from their sources in near real-time or in real-time. This data includes audio, video, sensors, web, images, social, and many other sources.

Hadoop attempts to manage big data elegantly by leveraging a series of tools to consume, manage, store, and proctor data.

So, what is Hadoop? Hadoop, in short, stands for Hadoop Distributed File System. Hadoop is an Apache project that includes HDFS, Yarn, Pig, Hive, Spark, ZooKeeper, Impala, and other components.

You can think of Hadoop as a RAID 1 for your data. When in a RAID 1 disk system, your data is spread equally across multiple drives, so no single disk becomes a point of failure; in Hadoop, data is spread across multiple nodes, so no one node becomes a single point of failure. Furthermore, in Hadoop, the loads and jobs are equally distributed across the nodes, thus providing great compute power at a fraction of the time.

As you progress through the world of data and analysis, more than likely, you will encounter data coming from big data systems. As a result, you must become familiar with these and their case of use and impact.

15

REPORTS AND ANALYSIS TYPES

Now that we have discussed amplitude data, data types, etc., as well as the type of analyses such as descriptive, predictive, and prescriptive. Let us now explore different types of reports and analyses beyond the basic three (3) classes.

Reports are the typical way by which people consume data and analyze results. As for reports go, there are many types. In this section, we will explore some of them and define cases of use. We will also examine types of analysis and case of use for such types of analysis.

Types of Reports

1. **Formal Reports** as very structured and focus on objectivity. Formal reports contain plenty of details. These reports delete any personal elements out of the reports and neutral language. Formal reports are usually used for internal and compliance reporting and to answer specific questions.

2. **Informal Reports** are typically concise. Informal reports do not follow a given structure and can be used to answer many different questions. Furthermore, informal reports generally are ad-hoc.

3. **Informative Reports** are reports that are typically highly visual and provide insight or data in a particular subject. These can be things such as expense or travel reports.

4. **Analytical Reports** are reports that lead to plausible decisions. Analytical reports

investigate multiple metrics and measures and usually provide what-if possibilities.

5. **Scheduled Reports** are reports that provide an outcome or output at a predictable frequency (schedule.) These reports can contain aspects of other report types but and always presented on that pre-defined frequency.

6. **Pixel Perfect Reports** are reports or outputs that must fit in each structure or format. Examples of these are pay stubs, invoices, and other forms of reports that meet a specific criterion and require repeatability in their configuration.

Types of Analysis

1. **Descriptive** are analyses that tell us what has taken place and is taking place. These do include all the types of reports described before.

2. **Exploratory** are analyses that summarize the primary data set attributes. These are statistical and allow you to explore data from summary to detail.

3. **Inferential** analyses are used to understand and infer the differences between properties. Furthermore, these analyses are used to test hypotheses as well as establishing possible estimates.

4. **Predictive,** as the name indicates, provides a predictive output or "what if" outputs based on conditions and scenarios. Predictive analyses do

not provide actual outcomes but possible outcomes. These analyses rely on historical data as well as user-provided scenarios.

5. **Casual** analyses are used to provide insights into cause and effect. These are used to find root cause analysis and use specific algorithmic and statistical methods.

6. **Mechanistic** analyses are used to examine how things are composed or engineered. These are typically used in complex industrial situations.

7. **Prescriptive** analyses provide a mechanism of what must be done. These differ from predictive as prescriptive give the recipe of what must occur, not just a possible outcome.

In addition to the already mentioned reports and analyses, there are variations of these that include:

- Decision Trees
- ANOVA
- Paired Test
- Kruskal Wallis Test
- Regression
- Linear
- Correlation

These types of analyses expand on those we already described. Each has specific cases of use with a particular output. In a later book, we will discuss each of these more in detail.

To summarize, reports and analyses are a crucial

component of a data and analytics practice. These will aid in telling a story behind the data and projecting the data in the correct format.

Always remember that reports are a form of analysis.

16

DATA & ANALYTICS CUSTOMERS

A critical component of effective data and analytical practice is working with, understanding, and dealing with customers. Customers can be external as well as internal but have a clear understanding of how to engage, identify, and service customers are crucial.

This chapter attempts to provide some context into identifying customers, collecting requirements, establishing timelines and deliverables, defining, and executing on test plan, deployment, and support.

Who are the customers?

Analytics and data customers come in all different forms. Customers range from functional (sales, claims, finance, human resources, marketing, etc.) to technical (call center/help desk, database group, systems, etc.)

For data and analytics projects, there are two (2) main categories of customers.

- Internal Customers
- External Customers

Internal customers work for or are directly affiliated with the business or your organization.

External customers use your product or services but are not directly affiliated with your division, group, or organization.

An example of an internal customer is your

internal HR department who makes data or analytics requests to the data management and analysis group or IT.

An example of an external customer is a customer who is asking for analytics data about consumer behavior for a specific business sector. In this case, the external customer is a different company using your services as a broker or syndicate.

Note that even within your organization, you may have internal and external customers.

Now let us discuss further customers. One key concern or consideration is if the customer is capable. So, what is a capable customer? A capable customer is a customer who can identify what they want and what they need, one who has reasonable expectations and most importantly is one who is cooperative.

If you do not have truly capable customers, you should focus on creating capable customers. To develop capable customers, you should commence by inquiring what is it that they need. What is required should be a "big picture," and from this picture, inquire further to isolate what is needed. Once you have asked what is the "big picture" ask then what has already been accomplished.

Ensure that both you and the customer understand what the customer seeks to do, when, and why. This level of understanding provides validation. The customer should always be challenged and validated as to what they need and why.

Finally, be sure to act as a facilitator, mentor, and coach for your customer. Attempt to provide some value assessment for the customer's requirements.

Now that we have identified customers and types of customers, we should now focus on requirements. How do we collect the requirements?

In most analytics projects, requirements tend to be ambiguous and broad.

For effective analytics, those requirements need to be captured and funneled with sufficient understanding.

To capture requirements effectively and efficiently, you should use a requirement funnel approach.

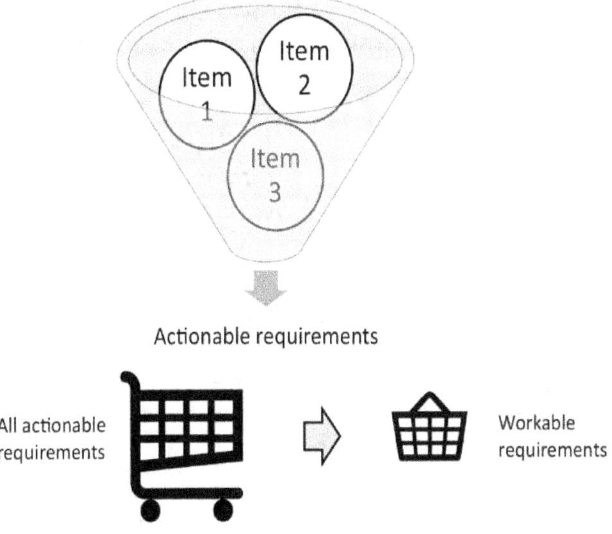

Figure 26

Figure 26 displays the requirements funnel approach. Here the customers list all possible requirements; in the process of asking what, when, where, who, and why you can isolate some truly actionable requirements. Once that process is complete, those requirements go into the requirements shopping cart. Beyond that, you should further reduce the scope into what is needed and actionable now. We will call those workable requirements. Those workable requirements will become your requirement shopping basket.

Once you have identified those, you must document those requirements into a Solutions Requirements Document (SRD) or Business Requirements Document (BRD.) These documents will indicate what is needed, who is required, what is in-scope, and what is out of scope.

BRD documents will be reviewed and agreed to by both the development team and the customer and will serve as a bilateral agreement with the parties.

One thing to remember with SRD's or BRD's is to have commencement and culmination dates for the work that will be done. Work should not be in perpetuity.

As part of the documentation and establishing the commencement and culmination dates, the timelines are in place. Timelines are sustainable, attainable, and appropriate periods that are defined to accomplish a task or objective.

Timelines should be tailored for different tasks and objectives. Timelines can be altered based on conditions that may influence them.

Timelines establish an expectation of delivery and accomplishment within a pre-determined period. Time expectations are fundamental in analytics and reporting as "time is of the essence."

All analytics, reporting, and data projects should have timelines. Depending on the project's scope and breadth, these timelines can be very short or long and define the project as an SLDC waterfall project or an Agile project.

Keep in mind that timelines should have sections and "Go" "No-Go" stages. These stages could be parts of a lifecycle or sprints as well.

One critical component of data and analytics project and project management is the concept of documentation and testing.

It is imperative that aside from documenting the requirements, each stage in the project has specific documentation. Documentation can include but should not be limited to:

1. Design Documents
2. ERD Diagrams
3. Wire Frames
4. Issues Logs
5. Architecture Diagrams and Documents
6. Resource Plan
7. Test Plans
8. Support Plan
9. User Documentation

Each of the documents listed above serves a specific purpose for the data and analytics projects. These will also aid in the continuous development and support of any solution.

One document that is perhaps the most critical is the test plan. The test plan should be in two (2) forms.

1. Integration/Development Test
2. User Acceptance Test

The core development team uses the integration and development test plan to ensure that the core functionality works as developed and designed. A test plan should be a pre-requisite before proceeding to User Acceptance Test.

The user community uses a user acceptance test

or UAT to ensure that the functionality, case of use, and business function work as expected by the user community. UAT is to be conducted and proctored by the lead on the user's side.

User acceptance testing must be a requirement before any data and analytics solutions are promoted to production.

17

NECESSARY KSA

So, what is a KSA? KSA is Knowledge, Skills, and Abilities. The initial question you may ask yourselves is, "Why do I need to care about KSA?" The second question is, "Why to do a skills assessment?" Especially if you already have a team in place and roles fulfilled. In preparation for a data and analytics initiative, doing a skills assessment is a way to determine if you even have the right business and technical resources/ Additionally, you want to assess if there are adequate resources to accomplish a new project's goals. KSA's will be pivotal in your project's success within the stipulated time, budget, and resources.

A skills assessment is also useful for handling your typical day to day ad-hoc questions. Do you find yourself always running at a deficit? Can you identify your bottlenecks? Perhaps it's a resource issue. Your team's skills assessment may identify required resources to staff your team to handle your day-to-day issues properly.

Along those lines, a skills assessment will help you see where the gaps are and opportunities to improve your team. A skills assessment can also build awareness for the team, and the new project initiative as to what resources may be required from other areas of the organization

A skills assessment can also see if there are needs in terms of hardware and software. Perhaps more resources can use an analytical tool like Tableau, but you only have 'x' number of licenses.

A skills assessment can also help with future staffing and resource requirements. Perhaps there is a deficiency with certain skills, and then the team can prepare by either training existing team members up or plan for hiring new members.

When looking for the essential skills your business analysts should have, you may be wondering to yourself if you ever need someone with business analyst type skills. Some shops may only have staffed their project teams with primarily technical developers. Whereas that might work for some work orders, for example, bug-fix, it is optimal to have either someone dedicated to the business analyst role or individuals with the requisite skills to take on some of those responsibilities. A project manager or lead, for example, can often have the skills listed below. Remember, the success of the BI initiative hinges on a partnership with IT and the business side. Here are some of the skills you can assess regarding this role:

1.   Analytical – the role must have the requisite analytical skills (some might say prowess) to understand the data required to answer the initiative's questions. Analytical skills are sometimes difficult to measure, but some things you might look for are, how well do you know the dataset asked of you, or will you be able to pick it up quickly? If given a task to analyze the dataset, would you provide insight into trends, outliers, and issues? Would you be able to figure out if the data looks incorrect or partially incorrect?

2.   Business – the role must have an adequate understanding of the functional or business side of the data.   Does the individual

understand the requirements concerning the overall organization and the departments' specific operational needs that will ultimately be the data consumer? Does the individual know the operational flow of the dataset required? Does the individual understand the business behind the numbers? For example, if dealing with general ledger information, does the user understand accounts' concepts and balance those accounts?

3. Query Ability – The role must have the ability to obtain and analyze the data on their own. Query ability will give the freedom to provide analysis outside of what the future report will provide. Query ability will enable the analyst the ability to do analysis on their own as well as give direction to the developers when it is needed.

4. Quality Assurance experience - The ability to test specific components and test the data itself in multiple ways. Testing is quite often an afterthought and not handled with the thoroughness and importance that it should be. Please ensure that testing techniques and plans are part of your list. You may even want to have dedicated testers who will handle this aspect.

5. Organizational Intelligence – The role should understand the organization as a whole and have access to the initiative's key stakeholders. Knowing who the ultimate users are and understanding their needs and

concerns are two different things. This role should provide a liaison function between the developer and business user of the product.

6. Technical domain knowledge – This role should have some of the common terminologies understood so that they may be able to communicate effectively with technological development and understand technical limitations when presented to them. For example, specific OLAP tools may have inherent limitations due to the tool's capabilities.

A technical developer role should have skills related to your specific project, team, department, and organization requirements.

Technical skills you might list are as follows:

1. Hardware – Does the individual have experience using Linux (what flavors? Redhat, Solaris, Ubuntu, Debian, etc.) Other platforms are there – Windows, of course, but there is also cloud infrastructure such as Amazon AWS or Microsoft Azure where you can host Linux and Windows's flavors.

2. Software:

    a. What IDE's are sanctioned by your organization? Eclipse, Visual Studio, and others are a few examples.

    b. What ETL tools are used in your

organization? SSIS, Informatica, Data Stage, Talent, and others.

c. What data replication tools are used in your organization? Shareplex, Attunity, GoldenGate, and others.

d. What databases are used? Oracle, MS SQL Server, Postgre, Netezza, MYSQL, etc.

e. What scripting languages? Java, .NET. Python, Ruby, C#, R, and others?

f. Is Big Data in use? Is this Cloudera, perhaps former Hortonworks HDP, HDFS, Yarn, Pig, Hive, Spark, Map Reduce, etc.

g. Is there source control? Git, SVN, CSV, Visual Source Safe, Team Foundation Server, etc.

Typically, an organization will have only one sanctioned source control, but this depends on the organization.

Non-Technical Skills:

a. Ability to unit test your code − provide testing scenarios and provide some testing of individually coded unit.
b. Business side − some fundamental understanding of the business − this makes unit testing above easier to do.

You may rely on a Project Manager or Business Analyst for Business Intelligence, Analytics, and Data projects in your organization. If this is the case, be it formally or informally, here are some of the areas you can assess:

1. Previous Project Management Experience - how many years or projects have you formally managed (PM role) regarding IT or BI initiatives. Is the individual PMI certified? (project management institute. PMBOK – global standards for projects – stands for Project Management Body of Knowledge.

2. Business Analysis experience – much like project management; how many years or projects have you formally participated in and been a BA. Does the BA have experience or exposure to the BABOK – global standards for business analysis – stands for Business Analysis Body of Knowledge.

3. Have you created and updated project plans from beginning to end? A plan can be divided into components, one of which is the schedule, and the other is the budget. Have you had experience doing either/both? Are you able to monitor and track projects according to the budget, deliverables, milestones?

4. Project management is highly administrative, so experience planning, coordinating, and running an efficient meeting is desirable. How much experience does this individual

have?

5. Project management also involves being a problem solver. Although the somewhat ambiguous term, understanding how to identify problems, address, mitigate, or resolve issues within a specific time frame is highly advantageous from a PM perspective. The ability to negotiate here is that the art of negotiation is useful when compromises are required.

6. Knowledge of the SDLC (systems or solutions development life cycle) and Agile methodologies is critical. Understanding different methodologies such as the waterfall are the most traditional to agile methods such as XP or Scrum.

7. A project manager must include proper test plans for the overall Project Plan. Experience with scheduling and resourcing comprehensive testing is pivotal to the success of the project.

Individuals with business, technical or PM roles may also need experience with organizational considerations such as governance practices utilized within your organization (e.g., HIPAA, SarbOx, GLBA, PCI. GDPR, FERPA, and others.)

If your organization has specific internal processes for handling daily work orders and issues/bugs, understanding usage, management, and workflow integration is essential. Some organizations use software such as JIRA or

Redmine to track issues.

COSO & COBIT have controlled frameworks that assist in providing structures and best practices concerning certain areas. COSO is the Committee of Sponsoring Organizations of the Treadway Commission and focused on controls for financial processes. COBIT (Control Objectives for Information and Related Technologies) is an open standard published by the IT Governance Institute and the Information Systems Audit and Control Association (ISACA). It is an IT control framework built in part upon the COSO framework.

ITIL (formerly known as Information Technology Infrastructure Library) is the most widely accepted approach to IT service management (ITSM).

Depending on your organization, you might also need to adhere to outside regulations such as HIPAA (Health Insurance Portability and Accountability Act of 1996.) These regulations dictate protection rules to individually identifiable health information, or Sarbox - Sarbanes-Oxley Act, a 2002 Federal law that set new accounting standards for publicly traded companies.

Understanding these rules and regulations is essential in avoiding fines and penalties and protecting your organization's data and public brand.

18

CORE
TERMINOLOGY

We use some common vocabulary or terminology for which we provide context and definitions here during this book.

Why would we need to learn common terminology?

One reason is the need to speak a common language between team members and professionals in this technology space. Speaking the same language will ensure everyone is on the same page and improve effective communication between all involved. Common terminology can also facilitate building a peer community where there can be continued encouragement, mutual support, and further education.

Another reason to familiarize yourself with these terms is to understand the concepts and principles behind those terms. One such example is the data modeling terms we will discuss later – understanding the idea behind these terms will undoubtedly be useful in the proper construction of your data warehouse solution.

Gaining familiarity with these terms will also lead to improved skills as you continue to speak and practice the concepts behind these terms.

A

Agent - An application that searches the data and sends an alert.

Aggregation - Information stored in a database in a summarized form.

Agile – Practice of development involves requirements, developing, and collaboration as part of a particular activity.

Alert - A message or notification sent automatically by a system when a particular condition occurs.

Attribute – Information included with a dimension or table that defines such a dimension or table.

Axis Dimension – See slicer dimension.

B

Business Intelligence – Technology that enables business users to see and use large amounts of complex data and act upon such data.

Business Performance Management - A set of processes and technologies required to manage and measure business activity performance with strategic and operational objectives. It can include the creation of dashboards, KPI's, and the use of communication tools. It is commonly used to measure how well or how poorly departments are doing.

C

Calculated Member(s) - Calculated members are often measures or data within a dimension or table that is calculated across levels (typically across a hierarchy)

Cells – This is the intersection of members where to

obtain data from.

Changing Dimensions - Tables and or dimensions that have levels) or attribute(s) of data that require to be updated frequently.

Conceptual Data Model - The highest-level ER model that includes the entities and the fundamental relationships between them.   No attribute or key information is included.

Conformed Dimensions – These are the dimensions used in more than one cube or area and are slow-changing, referred to as "Common Dimensions."

D

Dashboard - A dashboard is a portal containing summarized data designed to meet a particular responsibility's needs. Dashboards are also referred to as "Summary Pages."

Data Visualization - The presentation of data in a pictorial format such as a chart or map can be understood more easily.   Interactive visualization enables users to drill down or manipulate the graph to explore the data in further detail.

Data Engineer - A term that is gaining more traction these days – it refers to Individuals with both information technology and data experience. Data engineers are responsible for finding out, collecting, and organizing data for analysis. They are typically focused on building out systems, architectures, and platforms and can operationalize how data is used and leveraged in the organization. Skills required are domain experience with ETL, BI, big data tools, and coding languages such as SQL, python, ruby, pig, and hive. (note - for the uppercase acronyms, say the letters)

Data Mart - A database with the same characteristics as a data warehouse but is usually smaller and is focused on a particular subject or division; these are highly dimensional data elements.

Data Warehouse - A data warehouse is a collection of data extracted from one or more sources, is loaded into intelligent storage, and is optimized for business intelligence and reporting.

Data Scientist - This is another term gaining popularity. They are Individuals with mathematics and statistics backgrounds and will have some technical prowess as well. (Some may know basic scripting, for example.) They generally focus on finding new insights and building new models leveraging the data collected for them by data engineers.

Denormalization – Process used to optimize the read performance of a database by adding redundant data. Denormalized data typically requires many dimensions.

Dimension – A collection of data of the same type, allowing us to structure the multidimensional database. A dimension is sometimes referred to as an axis. In a measure, each cell of data is associated with one single position in each dimension. Time,

Location, and Product are classic dimensions.

DOLAP – Desktop OLAP is a small OLAP store for local multidimensional analysis on a user's desktop. There can be a mini multidimensional database or extraction of a data cube.

E

Entity Relationship Diagram (ERD) - A data model that describes the data or information aspects of a data model that can lend itself to building a data warehouse or data mart. The main components are entities (things) and the relationships that can exist among them. The three (3) kinds of models in data warehousing include Conceptual Data Model, Logical Data Model, and Physical Data model

ETL/ELT - Methods used to access and manipulate source data and load it into a data warehouse and another database.

F

Fact Table - Table which contains the individual facts being stored in the database used for reporting and calculations.

G

Granularity - The level of detail of the facts stored in a database table.

H

Hierarchy – Hierarchies are a series of parent-child

relationships that follow a normal flow, typically where a parent member represents the members' consolidation, which is its children. Hierarchies can be parent-child, skip level, level, and nested.

HOLAP (Hybrid OLAP) - A combined use of Relational OLAP (ROLAP) and Multidimensional OLAP (MOLAP).

I

INIT BLOCK (Initialization Block) – Block of code that is invoked upon initialization of the application.

K

KPI - Key Performance Indicators. They are measurable industry, department, or task-relevant performance metrics evaluated over a specified time and compared against acceptable norms, past performance, or targets. KPI measures the effectiveness of the business process in attaining that goal.

L

Logical Data Model - Includes detailed information about the entity, including attributes and relationships without going into the physical. The primary key is defined as well as all features for each entity. A foreign key is also established, and normalization occurs at each level.

M

Materialized View – This is a special kind of view, which physically exists inside the database (bound to the schema). It can contain joins and or aggregates and improve query execution time by pre-calculating joins and aggregation operations before execution.

MDX (Multi-Dimensional Expression) - A query language for retrieving and modeling data in OLAP cubes and OLAP based reports.

Measures - Measures, or facts, are typically additive data such as dollar value or quantity sold, and they can be specified in terms of the dimensions. For example, you might ask for the sum of dollars for a given product in each market over a given period.

Member - One of the data points for a level of a hierarchy of a dimension.

Metadata - Data that describes the data.

Metric – Another term for dimension.

MOLAP (Multi-Dimensional OLAP) – OLAP stores data and aggregations in multidimensional database structures such as Essbase or MS Analysis Services.

N

Navigation – Act to link reports from two or more distinct areas linked by a common member. Navigation is different than a hierarchy drill down because hierarchy drill-downs follow a regular flow of parent-child elements. Navigations can be used to link two or more elements/reports from different data sources, provided they have common linking elements of data.

Normalization - The process of organizing data following the rules of a relational database.

O

OLAP (Online Analytical Processing) – is used to analyze large quantities of data in real-time. OLAP functionality is characterized by multidimensional data elements with large data quantities and historical data analysis that supports business activities.

OLAP Cube – A multidimensional database that holds data more like a 3D spreadsheet than tables in a relational database. Cubes allow different views of the data to be quickly displayed.

OLTP (Online Transaction Processing) – OLTP uses computers to run the on-going operation of a business. OLTP systems include transactional databases.

Operational Datastore (ODS) - A database structure that is a repository for near real-time operational data rather than long term trend data. In some cases, it can be used to create tactical, operational reports, or as a staging area for a data warehouse or a data mart.

P

Physical Data Model - Includes all the data needed to build the model into the database management system physically. It Includes column name, column data types, foreign keys, primary keys, and indexes required.

The events that happen from logical to the physical data model are as follows:

1. Convert entities into tables.
2. Convert relationships into foreign keys.
3. Convert attributes into columns and
4. Modify the physical data model based on physical constraints/requirements.

Pivot Table – Summarization tool used to visualize data that allows sorting, grouping, filtering, and other functionality. Pivot tables can be found on Business Intelligence tools, spreadsheets, etc. Pivot tables are typically used against OLAP data sources.

R

RDBMS (Relational Database Management System) – This is the software used to store, access, and manage data.

Region – Component or area of a dashboard.

Repository – File where information is stored.

Report – Reports are summarized or transactional view of data in graph and table format.

ROLAP (Relational OLAP) – A form of Online analytical processing (OLAP) that performs dynamic multidimensional analysis of data stored in a traditional relational database rather than in a multidimensional database.

S

Schema - The logical organization of data in a database.

Scrum – A type of agile framework.

SDLC - Stands for solutions or systems development life cycle. It refers to the process of planning, building, and deploying systems.

Sets – This is a particular section of an OLAP cube identified by an alias, making it easier to query with MDX.

Shared Dimension - Dimensions that can be used by more than one cube (see Conformed Dimension).

Slicer Dimension – These dimensions are used to differentiate the cells' dimensions in the source cube of the query, indicated in the FROM clause, from the cells' dimensions in the resulting cube, which can be composed of multiple cube dimensions.

SQL (Structured Query Language) – Standard language for accessing relational databases.

Snowflake Schema - Logical arrangement of tables and or dimensions in a multidimensional database or OLAP cube resembling a snowflake in shape.

Sprint – A short-lived or short-timed period of activity for teams to complete work. Typically, part of an Agile and Scrum process.

Star Schema - A database design that consists of a fact table and one or more dimension tables.

SVOT - The technical concept describing a centralized data warehouse that stores data in a non-redundant form that becomes the source for the rest of the organization for that piece of information

T

Tuples – Uniquely identify a section of an OLAP cube.

U

UAT - Stands for User Acceptance Testing. It refers to a stage in the SDLC testing where target users can - sign off on the product ready for deployment.

V

View – Database query accessible as a virtual table. Unlike tables and materialized views, views are not bound to the database physical schema.

By no means are all the terms used in data and analytics practices covered here. The terms covered here should serve as a good starting point.

INDEX

K

L

M

N

O

P

Z

ZooKeeper, 101

ABOUT THE AUTHOR

Daniel O'Connell is an Information Technology Executive, entrepreneur, and the founder of DocLogical, LLC. He has held executive positions in Agricultural Technology, Higher Education, Aerospace and Defense, and Software and Technology industries. Additionally, Daniel is a professor teaching data science and computer science at the undergraduate and graduate levels. An active practitioner of Data Science, Data Architecture, and Analytics. Daniel has over 20 years of experience in Information, pioneering many data governance initiatives, data science, data warehousing, and data visualizations.